Going Bridal

How to Get Married Without Losing Your Mind

Li Robbins

Contemporary Books

Chicago New York San Francisco Lisbon London Madrid Mexico City
Milan New Delhi San Juan Seoul Singapore Sydney Toronto

Library of Congress Cataloging-in-Publication Data

Robbins, Li.
    Going bridal : how to get married without losing your mind / Li Robbins.
       p.   cm.
    ISBN 0-07-142612-4
    1. Weddings—Planning.   2. Brides—Psychology.   3. Stress management for
women.   I. Title.

HQ745.R62   2004
395.2'2—dc22   2003023541

This book is dedicated to my husband, James Cullingham,
who (almost!) never made me Go Bridal.

1 2 3 4 5 6 7 8 9 0 AGM/AGM 2 1 0 9 8 7 6 5 4 3

ISBN 0-07-142612-4

This book is printed on acid-free paper.

CONTENTS

ACKNOWLEDGMENTS

I'D LIKE TO RAISE MY GLASS (filled with Dom Perignon, of course) to the brides (and a few good grooms) who contributed their stories, insights, woes, and wishes to this book. Ideally I'd thank you each by name, but as promised . . . all names have been changed to protect the guilty.

A heartfelt thanks goes to my extraordinarily positive two-woman cheering team: my agent, Jackie Joiner, and editor, Michele Pezzuti.

Kudos again to all of the people who helped shape my own wedding. Friends, family, and pros alike who toasted, decorated, greeted, strummed, photographed, laughed, cried, cooked, served, sang, created, and cleaned up . . . and rarely made me Go Bridal. (When they did, why, it was only because they wanted to provide me with a book idea.)

I'd also like to say thank you to the following for their assistance with *Going Bridal*—either in real life or with the prose edition. Alphabetically from A to V: Mary Ambrose for smart early morning suggestions when this book was just a twinkle. "My friend Stephanie" (Conn), who understands the therapeutic benefits of hair talk. James Cullingham, my incredibly supportive and Long-Suffering Husband. Sarah Cullingham, for handling with such good grace the writer "Going Bridal" in our home. Annette Cullingham and Scott Jameson, for providing Lake Joe writer's retreat. Emily

Donaldson, for being a consistent cyber pal and wiseass. Darcelle Hall, for understanding the need to "peel back the emotional layers," and for accepting my wedding shoes. Ana Harland, for always writing back with something to say. Walter and Phyllis Robbins, for having an inspirational marriage, and for seeming unfazed that after all was said and done . . . I was finally tying the knot. Jim Robbins, for never dreaming of toasting our engagement with anything other than the best champagne. Wendy Robbins, for (always) standing up for me, and for having the perspective to make me laugh off a near–Going Bridal episode minutes before my wedding, thus eliminating the possibility of an outbreak. And Josey Vogels, for her tangible help re the book-publishing biz, and her emotional support, demonstrated so fabulously through her indefatigable quest for what became the prewedding mantra: "Gitch, shawl, slip, 'n' shoes."

A toast to you all!

INTRODUCTION

LIKE SO MANY LITTLE GIRLS, I'd dreamed of it. Imagined myself walking down the aisle, radiant with joy on the happiest day of my life. Wondering who would be at the other end to meet me in that moment of ultimate bliss. What would he look like? Would he be . . . a dapple gray? A chestnut? Perhaps a palomino?

Yes, it's true, the only aisle I ever pictured walking down was the one in the middle of a barn. I never secretly fantasized about parading along the wedding route, Dad in tow. Admittedly once I grew up (after my parents finally sprang for the palomino) and entered the world of boy meets girl, I did have dreams of a Mr. Compassionate/Smart/Funny and so on, but those dreams still didn't end with saying, "I do." True, there were boyfriends—good, bad, and indifferent—but none that inspired me to ponder with any real intent the idea of marriage, let alone a wedding.

Years passed. Then along came the man to whom this book is dedicated. My feelings for him were unexpected, different, new, deeper, and (what a stroke of luck) mutual. We planned to wed.

At first blush, planning our wedding looked like a walk in the park. (Literally, given we had the whole thing figured out in half an hour on one sunny park-walking day.) It would be intimate—forty people tops. (OK, so we had seventy.) Held someplace fun, comfy, and cheap. (A friend's restaurant—all of the above.) With a nonreligious ceremony. (Delivered by a therapist and former minister who brought the house down with her conviction and wisdom.) The day was a blur of hugs, tears, laughter, and smeared lipstick—which I never bothered to reapply because I didn't want to miss a minute of our wedding. Sure, there were details we glossed over ("Oh yeah, there is a cake that needs to be cut, isn't there?") and things that went slightly awry (how *did* the ceremony become twice as long as planned?). But nothing on the day of the wedding made (lucky) me Go Bridal.

No, that came earlier. It happened in small ways over small things. For example, over what my friends and I called the foundation garments. (You try finding a ready-made slip that works under a sheer, ivory, bias-cut knee-length dress.) And again over division of labor with my darling fiancé, and once or twice more when various members of Team Wedding had ideas that differentiated somewhat from ours. But the day I came face-to-face with full-blown Going Bridal was over that most clichéd of wedding disasters: The Ring.

Here's the back story. The rings had been ordered through an artisan's gallery well in advance (possibly the only thing that was done well in advance), to be made by a talented artist on the other side of the country. (Yes, I know, but that's where the talented artist happened to live.) Instead of showing up on the designated day, the rings were late. First by a day, then another, eventually by a matter of weeks. Now just two weeks shy of the wedding, I was a little on edge when we were told the rings had finally arrived. Husband-to-be and I made tracks posthaste, eagerly entering the gallery only to discover the clerk was extremely busy with other customers. Turned out she was on her own that day, due to the illness of a colleague. Did I care? On an intellectual level, perhaps. But on an emotional level I felt something akin to fury as she slowly served these other, lesser beings, who were just shopping after all, not there to try on their WEDDING RINGS. When at last (perhaps heeding my drumming fingers on the countertop, or the clearly visible pulse leaping beneath my eye) she slipped the rings onto our fingers, mine (yup, you guessed it) went up to about my knuckle. Also was the wrong width. Also didn't have the artist's design as discussed at length, months prior.

I confess I came perilously close to tears. (OK, so maybe a little sniveling took place.) The gallery clerk hastened to describe in calm, empathetic detail all the methods by which she would ensure a new handcrafted ring would be miraculously made (again) and flown across the country in time. But I could feel myself resisting her attempts at rational discussion, disregarding her soothing words. I had a strong urge to grab her by the scruff and say, "Listen, lady, I want that ring here and I want it now. No more excuses, got it?" Instead I allowed my fiancé to tactfully shepherd my somewhat shaky self out the door, onto the street. As other pedestrians scurried away from the scene of the crime, I realized my agitation was absolutely wedding-specific, far beyond what I considered my normal, fairly reasonable reaction to life's curveballs. I realized I was in the grip of something bigger than you or me. I realized I was . . . Going Bridal.

Meanwhile, on the other side of town, I had several friends who were also in various stages of planning their weddings. Each of these women was smart, funny, loving—your basic stable human being. And yet as time went by, they all exhibited signs of the same malady I'd witnessed in myself. Not, thankfully, over any ring crisis, but over sundry other wedding matters. Relatives who behaved in a less-than-sensitive manner, menu plans that looked like menu catastrophe theories, venues being singularly uncooperative, dresses that refused to be located, and so on and so on. And these same women who at their jobs controlled, variously, large numbers of people, large sums of money, large creative visions, all became mad as hatters at various stages along the bridal path. "Going Bridal," I'd think to myself, whenever one of them would recount the latest.

Soon I began hearing of other, similar cases, brides who were friends of friends of friends. "Yup, there's another one Going Bridal," I'd say, upon hearing of yet another woman having a stand-off with some member of her wedding flock. The phenomenon was fascinating. Especially given that the nature of the bridal beast was so very similar from case to case. Only the particulars—the players and the stage—differed.

Yet I didn't buy the prevailing theory that women Going Bridal were simply narcissistic, wedding-obsessed kooks. For one thing, clearly part of the problem was the unpleasantly steep learning curve a woman faces when encountering the tentacles of the wedding industry for the first time. For another, it wasn't just women who were frothing at the mouth over some idealized wedding day. There were many other frothers: family, friends, strangers, and the fiancé.

It seemed to me that weddings, for all their potential to draw people together in love, generosity, and creativity, were also remarkable catalysts for discord and emotional upheaval. Brides simply happened to be at the center of this real-life drama. Because even in these post-postmodern times it still holds true that if anyone in the wedding planning saga typically occupies control central (or lack of control central, depending), it most frequently is she.

Women planning to marry are, consequently, cast into the trying dual roles of patient, struggling with symptoms of stress and emotional overload, and doctor, the mediator for all the emotional brouhaha spilling over from everyone else involved. You may ask yourself why weddings—celebratory events, after all—turn out to be such incubators for all this gnashing and wailing. But think on it. Typically weddings are simultaneously a party, a rite of passage, a gathering of most significant people, an exalted moment rising above the humdrum of daily life—organizing such an event might understandably cause a little stress, wouldn't you agree?

I figured brides needed help. Not with matters of wedding to-dos, but with matters of the heart. It seemed to me that sharing the experiences of a number of savvy brides (along with my own hopefully insightful observations) would be a useful drop in that help-needed bucket. Postwedding clarity makes it ever so much easier to see where a bride goes wrong, where she goes right, and where she Goes Bridal. Why let this store of bridal lore go for naught? And at the very least, women embroiled in wedding planning can always use a much-needed laugh. Thus the idea for *Going Bridal: How to Get Married Without Losing Your Mind*.

When I look back on my own Going Bridal revelation, via the fateful day of The Ring Not Fitting, I realize there was one thing that saved me, and that was naming my condition. Going Bridal—as a concept—made me laugh. And of course laughter immediately diminished the symptoms. It was an instant reminder of the value of humor and perspective, two items all too frequently in dangerously short supply leading up to W-Day.

My fiancé and I actively cultivated the two. After any wedding planning "differences" we would get over ourselves, laugh, and agree, "But no matter what, we *will* enjoy the final week leading up to the wedding, right?" And we did. When we got to that appointed hour, we set all angsting aside. Even with some of the details still in limbo. (For instance, THE RING, which finally showed up three days before!)

Announcing this marvelous achievement of ours might seem the height of annoying smugness, so I should point out that reaching the goal of near-serenity was not without effort. For me it meant taking an infinite number of deep breaths; employing useful mantras (such as "Details not important, details not important"); and other necessary mind-over-matter strategies. It helped to recall (again and again) what it was I wanted my wedding to be—a celebration with family, friends, new husband (and even a stranger or two). I was fairly certain that "celebration" and "Going Bridal" were mutually exclusive.

So yes, all that breathing, humor, and perspective stuff meant hard emotional work at times (perhaps not unlike marriage itself), but it paid off, big-time. There was something deeply satisfying in truly accepting that the whole wedding thing was about love, not whether the toasts happened at 18:08:30 or 19:00 hours.

And now a word about the focus of this book. It deals mostly with Western world "white wedding" traditions. (Although given the subject is weddings, the triggers to the condition are fairly universal: family, friends, strangers . . . and the fiancé.) It's also unabashedly heterosexual, but I dare say that couples planning same-sex unions might find that some of these triggers and treatments apply. The reason for this focus is a practical one: so many stories, so little space.

Even within this context there are many specific wedding scenarios that are not included. Why? Because there are so darn many! Ask any married man or woman, "What was your wedding like?" and you'll find a cache of wedding-related anecdotes, simultaneously unique and universal. In this book I've tried, albeit with tongue in cheek, to offer at least a sampling of possible ways to deal with a sampling of possible situations.

Finally, a note about the fictional story that begins each chapter, a tale of one woman and her friends Angela, Edie, and Priya. These characters bear no resemblance to any person, living or dead, et cetera. (OK, so the protagonist may have had dreams of a Thoroughbred, but otherwise, no resemblance.) No, it was just a fancy of mine to let at least one woman play out her wedding drama from beginning to end in this book. Because after all, what is the story of Going Bridal without . . . The Bride?

I

And You Thought PMS Was Bad

A Tale of Going Bridal,
as Told by Definitely-Not-the-Bride

If, for some depraved reason, you want to drive a woman insane, simply give her a wedding to plan. Preferably her own. This is my current theory, based on the crazed states I've witnessed some of my nearest, dearest, and formerly sane friends enter into since getting engaged.

I have three, count 'em, three friends getting married this year. There's Edie, who until what seems like yesterday wasn't even sure if she wanted to be in a relationship, let alone get married. Then there's Angela, who's been living with this guy for a dog's age (and sadly he's a bit of a dog himself), finally announcing she's "persuaded" him to tie the knot. And Priya, who's gone 360 and isn't doing the arranged marriage thing she claimed to want since age dot. No, she's marrying the love of her life. (Let's see, I think she's known him for all of five months now?)

In the past we've been the kind of good friends who are extremely supportive of each other but still have frequent, how shall I put it, "differences." Resulting in more than one occasion where

someone's huffed off, thus providing fodder for lengthy reconcilia-
tory follow-ups. Of course, now the bridal buddies have so much
more material for all the highs and lows. They spend hours gleefully
scooping each other on place-setting innovations, exploring their
mutual dislike of veils, carping about the others' wedding budgets.

As for me? I'm happily living with my man, trying to ignore the
whole thing. Hah. *Trying* is the operative word. Short of telling all
of them, "I don't wanna come out and play wedding," there's no
ignoring the W-Day lunacy. And we're talking full-scale, out-of-
their-collective-tree cuckoo.

Take last weekend, for example. Edie calls me to get together for
cocktails. She doesn't mention the "W" word once. Great, I think,
like old times. I meet her at our favorite watering hole, which funnily enough I've never noticed is just down the street from Unique
Wedding Dresses for the Original Bride. After Edie's plied me with
two of the pink ones I foolishly agree "just to look." (Although not
without muttering something about that ultimate oxymoron, "Original Bride.")

"Edie," I say, after fingering what seems to be a five-thousand-
dollar hunk of shiny but otherwise unremarkable dress, "Think how
many decades of pink drinks this would buy. Besides, isn't five thou-
sand dollars a little more than you earn in three months at your non-
profit independent-video-collective job?" But I've lost her; she's
wafting deeper into the silken racks. And all the while the woman
responsible for corralling Unique Wedding Dresses is watching Edie
with this scary fixed smile on her face. She's a spider and the satin,
silk, lace, and oh-so-charmingly-named zibeline is her web.

Just as I'm thinking I should drag Edie out by her bridal boots
the cell rings. Thank God it's Angela, who wonders if I'd like to pop
by for a bit of sloth. "You betcha," I say, hightailing out of Original
Bride–land, leaving Edie and the spider cooing over something called
an illusion sleeve.

I arrive at Angela's to find her skulking outside her building. Seems that Dog Boy (a pet name for him I don't share with Angie, oddly enough) is home and she doesn't want him to overhear our conversation. So instead of curling up on the sofa and watching mindless TV as advertised, we end up in an absurdly expensive chichi joint she says she really, really needs to check out as a possibility for her reception. Although as it happens she isn't entirely sure if there will be a reception, because Dog Boy's mother, who was going to foot the bill for the whole thing, is threatening to renege, saying she'd rather cater the wedding in her living room—half a continent away. Worse, Dog Boy is sticking up for The Mom.

In the midst of telling me this Angela (previously known as "bust your chops" Angela) starts to cry and go on about how Her Day will be ruined if they can't book something like this absurdly expensive chichi joint. I point out to her that until a month ago she didn't even have something called "Her Day," which only makes her turn on me, hissing, "You can't understand, you're not getting married."

"Ohhhhh-kayyyyy," is about the only response I can muster, eyes rolling, but she barrels on, oblivious to any insult, and continues to catalogue her woes. She's heard Edie is scoping Unique Wedding Dresses and she's pissed, since she went there first and their tastes are so similar. (Untrue, but I think this is perhaps not the best time to point it out.) She really doesn't like the guy Dog Boy wants as best man. I know and she knows that she really doesn't like him because she slept with him once (pre–Dog Boy), but her darling fiancé doesn't know that. She's convinced (rightly) that having Mr. Bad-One-Night-Stand near the altar will make her tense on Her Day. Next in the litany, her sisters who are campaigning to be bridesmaids despite knowing she isn't planning on having any. She's thinking instead of having all the women attending the wedding (all thirty-five of them) surge forward to surround her for a huge girly hug before the ceremony, which she thinks is a cool twist on the bridesmaid idea. But Dog Boy (bless him for once) thinks this would be ridiculous.

After forty minutes of this she drags her sorry bridal butt home, and I limp off in the other direction. Home sweet home. I turn the key in the lock; the phone is ringing and I dash for it, hoping for some rational adult conversation.

"It's Priya," she says, and before I can even say "Hey-how's-it-going" she continues, "My mother just told me, again, that she might not come to the wedding after all." And bursts into tears. As do I. (Well it's either that or laugh, right?)

THE CONDITION OF GOING BRIDAL, UP CLOSE AND (VERY) PERSONAL

Some poor souls believe there are actually three things in life that are certain: death, taxes, and if you're a woman planning your wedding—Going Bridal. It's an understandable conclusion, given it cannot be denied that Going Bridal is a state of mind many brides find difficult to avoid. Furthermore, the condition is hardly without cause—after all, who wouldn't get a trifle tense in the midst of planning a ritual/celebration/party/rite of passage that quivers with significance for both planner and many a plannee? It is precisely this confluence of heightened emotional state and potential logistical nightmare that causes many women to Go Bridal.

Fortunately, certain aspects of the condition are easily grasped. For instance, we do know that Going Bridal is wedding-specific. There is no shortage of evidence indicating that if left unchecked, Going Bridal results in an emotional cyclone unlike any other. Less fortunately, this evidence points to the following sorry conclusion: if permitted to flourish without reductive treatments, Going Bridal may run rampant, manifesting itself in any number of less-than-pleasant permutations and combinations. In its darkest hour Going Bridal has been known to turn intelligent, competent, together women into excitable divas; in its bleakest, into demoralized, weepy shadows of their former selves.

Much empathy for sufferers of the condition is to be gained by recognizing that Going Bridal is an uninvited temporary illness. It sneaks up on its unsuspecting victim, and suddenly the happy bride-to-be is running a fever. Therefore it is essential to acknowledge that except in extreme cases, it is not that the bride is reverting to brat-in-temper-tantrum mode. Diagnosis of most cases will reveal a complex of triggers that incite the state, rather than a single bride-originated source.

Consequently, if a woman is seen to be Going Bridal to any significant degree you must restrain yourself from pointing the finger solely in her direction, thus blaming it on the bride. (Tempting as it may be, particularly since "blame it on the bride" has such a nice ring to it.) Indeed, nine out of ten therapists at Going Bridal World Headquarters assure brides who feel that they are lesser beings for occasionally losing their marbles over wedding planning that they needn't wallow in post–Going Bridal guilt. Because in the final analysis, Going Bridal is a multipronged condition, with some of the sharpest prongs sculpted to a fine point by others. You know those others—the family, the friends, the perfect strangers, and the fiancé? Frequently all of these fine people are seen to exhibit a low-grade form of the same ailment, and act as triggers to the full-blown condition.

The good news is this. In cases where Going Bridal has been treated and controlled, it is far from dire. In these cases Going Bridal merely becomes the stuff of "One day we'll look back on this and laugh." This scenario is to be aspired to. What's more, it is readily cultivated by actively applying the treatments suggested in the pages of this book.

WE'RE SO DISGUSTINGLY HAPPY

Going Bridal is far away from the thoughts of most of the newly engaged. In truth, the bride and her betrothed frequently are so thrilled with their plan to marry that they cannot imagine the difficulties that lie in wait. To Going Bridal survivors this may seem quaint. The newly engaged may appear as innocents, wandering haplessly into a maze of demanding and needy family and friends, skipping into an illusory garden where unpredictable and inconsiderate strangers lurk, just waiting to ignore phone calls about dress fittings or menu options. In short, the happy couple may start out in a state of giddy oblivion, heedless of the challenges involved in creating the significant event known as The Wedding. This, of course, will not last.

It's one of life's peculiar little ironies that many brides (not to mention their friends, family members, coworkers, indeed, passing acquaintances) recognize the existence of Going Bridal, and yet perpetuate the strange reluctance to deal with the condition. The prevalent attitude has been to assume (or hope and pray) it will pass with the signing of the register. But why must brides and co. suffer so? Whether it is six weeks or six years from "Yes" to "I do," it is still time that could be best spent cultivating a state of mind that doesn't involve either chronic moping, 4 A.M. angst, or occasional and seemingly irrational hissy fits. It could be a time of genuine delight and excitement, where both the petty planning-related annoyances and challenging interpersonal relationships are only a part of the equation. A time when health and happiness duke it out triumphantly against trauma and melodrama.

Which is not to deny that planning a significant event is without its inherently trying moments. (Ever tried hosting a friend's surprise party or your parents' anniversary do?) But the operative word here is "moments," not "eons."

Treatment or Trauma? The Choice Is Yours

Treating the condition is essential because if allowed to develop, Going Bridal has the potential to sully the experience of planning what is, after all, meant to be a joyous occasion. (As well as potentially savaging relations with friends, family, and quite possibly the fiancé along the way.)

What a Bride Needs

- A sense of purpose. (Translation: the marriage is the purpose, not the wedding.)
- A sense of occasion. (Achievable with two people and a preacher man—it's all in the attitude, not in the sizzle.)
- A sense of proportion. (You know that crowning-of-heads-of-state thing called a coronation? This ain't it. Think *celebration*, not *coronation*—once more, *celebration*, not *coronation*.)

What a Bride Gets (When Going Bridal)

- A sense of STRESSSSSS!
- A sense of ANGSSSSST!
- A sense of DOOOOM!

Of course you could take the path of greatest avoidance. Some couples opt to elope or refuse to get married at all in a desperate attempt to avoid Going Bridal—they've seen some of their loved ones fall prey to the full-on throes of the condition. That's well and good if they are at peace with their choice. But if it's a sorry second to what they really want, it seems a shame that what stands between the couple and their wedding is merely the fear of Going Bridal.

What are we to conclude from all of this? One thing is certain— clearly, brides need help. Not with choosing the china pattern, but with keeping sane while someone else doggedly tries to influence their choice. Not with figuring out whether the bridesmaids will be in taffeta, satin, or scuba-diving gear, but with figuring out what to say when some ancient friend from the past gets in a twist because she wasn't asked to be among The Chosen Few. Help is at hand— you might want to look upon this book as something of a planner for your wedding psyche.

"BUT I'M NOT *THAT* KIND OF BRIDE!" (OH YEAH?)

One might suppose that Going Bridal is restricted to brides who choose to have fairly traditional weddings, involving all of the typical North American white wedding trappings: the bridal shower(s), the matching outfits, the infinitely pointless but pleasing favors nestled beside the thoughtfully crafted place settings, and so forth and so on—the details of which are prescribed, but with multiple, minute, and potentially maddening variations. (Will that be the adorable bride and groom magnet, or the "love you forever" key chain? The artful organic sunflower and pinecones arrangement, or the forced marigolds dipped in rosewater? The Cupid mega-tiara, or the pearl and rhinestone bun wrap? Argh!)

Conversely, one might suppose that a woman choosing to create a wedding with little if any adherence to these traditions would be exempt from Going Bridal. Not so. Without a doubt many a bride chooses an alternative path, sometimes dispensing altogether with such concepts as bridesmaids, the vows, the bubbly. (Although we hope not the bubbly, c'mon, not the bubbly . . .)

It's also true that nowadays couples at all stages of life decide to marry, frequently paying for their weddings themselves. These couples are likely fully aware of their ability to decide what they do and do not want in a wedding, as in all aspects of life. They don't need advice on whether monogrammed golf balls make a better favor for their guests than personalized voodoo dolls. (Although the latter might suit some guests just fine, the ones who are completely "up-to-here" with all things wedding by the time the day finally rolls around.)

Thus it is entirely possible that a woman's Going Bridal tendencies are not an issue of her tender unformed identity. There's a good possibility she is quite capable of figuring out what she wants, thank you very much, and feels no need to consult treatises on "personalizing your wedding." That's because she knows she'll have "a wedding to remember." After all, it's hers! Still, no matter how savvy the bride, no matter how conventional or not the setting may be, there are predictable emotions and issues stirred up from the moment of the announcement to the moment of "I do." Emotions, when wedded (so to speak) to the seemingly bottomless logistics pit of wedding planning, become quite capable of making both trad bride and nonconformist bride alike . . . Go Bridal.

SELF-ASSESS YOUR GOING BRIDAL POTENTIAL

Let's just say you're thinking about getting married but haven't made the decision yet, or you're still trying to choose between suitors or some such. (Actually if it's the latter scenario forget it, you're in deeper trouble than Going Bridal.) Or perhaps you're engaged but it's still early in your preplanning, planning-to-plan days. You may want to administer the following self-assessment to see if you have any vulnerabilities that could render you a victim of Going Bridal.

1. Are you a bride-to-be? (If the answer's yes, you definitely are vulnerable.)
2. Does the thought of organizing a party/dinner/event/celebration/ceremony/rite of passage involving your closest friends and significant family members make you even a tiny bit nervous? (If the answer's yes, you could Go Bridal.)

3. Are you the kind of woman who doesn't give a toss about how she looks or what she's wearing when she's the center of attention? (If the answer's no, you may be en route to Going Bridal.)

4. Do you like it when the people you love start snarling like irate caged animals and coming at you with all their "issues" about each other? (If the answer is no, Going Bridal is a possibility in your life.)

5. Have you taken a look at your comfy self and suddenly started making secretive confessional calls to personal trainers or weight-loss clinics? (If the answer's yes, Going Bridal could be in your future.)

6. However traditional or nontraditional you are, do you expect, assume, or demand your wedding day will be summed up by that lofty, terrifying word, *perfect*? (If you say yes to this one your goose is cooked, sister. You will definitely run afoul of Going Bridal.)

DIAGNOSING EARLY SYMPTOMS OF GOING BRIDAL

Let's say you're recently engaged. Congratulations! It's a lovely state of mind, isn't it. No? If your answer was a tearful "Not really," it could be that's because you're already Going Bridal. You might want to pause and take the following test to verify if indeed you are exhibiting Going Bridal symptoms.

Self-Assess Early Symptoms of Going Bridal

After you said yes (or after he said yes, given there are some swell dames who do the asking), have you exhibited any of the following symptoms?

1. You're thinking about the crucial elements of the wedding (where, when, who, how) and you start to feel any of the following: short of time, short of money, short of breath.

2. Talking to your friends about the wedding is great fun until one of them shows less than 100 percent interest, causing you to feel a distinct urge to regress to earlier, childhood ways. (Translation: you feel like pinching her, hard.)

3. You like to moon about dreamily "talking wedding" with your fiancé, but lately he keeps saying, "How much is this going to cost us?" and evil responses along the lines of "Whatsamatta, you a cheapskate or something?" flood your mind.

4. You haven't done a thing yet about the date, the photographer, the venue, let alone The Dress, but instead of following your plan to spring out of bed early to begin organizing, you pull the covers up over your head and contemplate calling in sick to work. Again.

5. Your mother is trying to organize a family reunion and your response is, "What, in the same *year* as my wedding? How could you?"

6. The wedding comes to mind with increasing frequency and you find yourself feeling something you don't typically associate with happiness, something that reminds you of that useful expression "fight or flight." Why, could that be . . . fear?

DIAGNOSING THE QUEST FOR PHYSICAL PERFECTION–INDUCED GOING BRIDAL: THE SYMPTOMS, THE TRIGGERS, THE TREATMENTS, THE GOALS

OK, so now you know Going Bridal could be in your future, or perhaps even your present. It's time to take a quick look at how the condition can arise, through one of the all-time Going Bridal triggers. You must imagine the following in 1940s epic movie font with accompanying overblown music: THE QUEST . . . FOR PHYSICAL PERFECTION.

Symptoms of the Quest for Physical Perfection–Induced Going Bridal

- You start spending inordinate amounts of time naked in front of the mirror contemplating the previously inconceivable notions of dieting and/or wearing foundation garments containing heinous devices known as "control panels."
- You pull out the ancient photos and repeatedly ask your friends if they don't think you look far better at a womanly thirty-four than you did in those annoyingly sexy shots of you at a girlish twenty-one.
- You up your gym program from your normal thrice-weekly routine to every day, twice a day. (That is excepting weekends, when you participate in six-hour Workoutaholics Anonymous Cardio Overloadathons.)
- You stare at your favorite luscious cream cheese and lox bagel and instead of thinking, "Yum!" you ponder, "Does cellulite show through silk?" and refuse to take a bite.
- Your hairdresser tells you she is suddenly moving from New York City to New Never-Heard-of-It, and instead of graciously thanking her for all her years of dealing with your impossibly curly locks you say, "Surely you could wait to move *there* until after my wedding?"
- You look at your recently acquired and very beautiful wedding dress and find yourself saying to it, "Geez, I think you're just too good for me, baby."

The Trigger: I Must Look Fabulous on My Wedding Day

"I always thought I was pretty comfortable in my body, didn't diet and didn't obsess, at least most of the time," says Katie, a recent bride who had a close encounter with this insidious trigger. "But when we decided to have a big wedding and I bought this beautiful, close-fitting, sleeveless dress, I got caught up in obsessing about how I was going to look in it. Especially since I actually bought the dress kind of impulsively right after getting engaged, and then put on a few pounds in the postengagement spree." Katie, although clearly embarrassed to admit it, ended up losing so much weight before her wedding that the slightly snug dress became tentlike as The Day approached. "It was ridiculous—from one extreme to the other. I was hell-bent on looking great at the wedding, even though rationally I knew looking great didn't mean skinny. But I just lost perspective. In the end my sister convinced me to have an emergency alteration done two days before the wedding. It was an improvement, but it still bugs me that on my wedding day the gown really didn't hang properly."

How many times have you gone out thinking you want to look your best for that major soiree, big job interview, hot date, your best friend's book launch, only to have the typical forms of sabotage arise? (The zit, the proverbial bad hair day, the curse of overlooked visible panty line, the last-year's-pants-on-this-year's-butt . . .) Well, chances are that at least one irritant of this sort may come along to undermine your vision of wedding day Absolute Beauty. Sure, you'll look great. But shocking as it may be to contemplate, you won't necessarily look your most fabulous you. (Rest assured though, you will be radiant—that's the wonderful thing about happiness.) So if the I Must Look Fabulous trigger takes the form of angsting over various body parts and their perceived flaws (the delicate wobble of the upper arms, the recent spreading of the southern hemisphere, whatever), it is essential that you apply one of the following treatments ASAP.

The Treatment: Get a Grip

The Goal: So that you are not constantly in some ravenous, cranky, and poisonous frame of mind in the days leading up to your wedding, believing your only true friends are the people you previously called the Get-a-Life gang who live at the gym.

The Application: Yes, you want to look good, and yes, if the bias-cut gown you're thinking about purchasing won't discreetly conceal your burgeoning midsection you may want to consider a different style. Yes, if the ten truly unnecessary pounds you've packed on by constant consumption of Death by Chocolate while watching the idiot box makes you uncomfortable in your own skin, you may want to reduce said consumption, and perhaps take up walking. But this is not the stuff of catastrophe. You will, after all, be surrounded by people who care about you, and they're not going to be thinking, "Man oh man, she never should have worn that tight yellow number, not with her sallow skin and obesity issues." (And if they are, let's hope they're not invited to your anniversary party.) Of course it's entirely understandable you want to look lovely, but (really!) it isn't the defining moment of the century. Consequently it behooves a bride to self-administer this treatment at regular intervals, particularly during dress fittings. However, if you do want to dust yourself off that couch and take up some bride-to-be renovations, carefully consider the following treatment.

Additional Treatment: "Reasonable Regime"

This treatment may sound like a contradiction—after all, think of the word that most commonly precedes regime—would that be . . . fascist? However, let's take a boo at the notion of creating a prewedding plan for fitness, eating well, skin care, and so on. Naturally it would be best if you already have these elements in place. (We call that "being healthy.") But if not, there's no sense punishing a lifetime of bad or indifferent habits with a sudden onslaught of intense scrutiny and attempted reconditioning. Why? Because it won't work, and it will make you . . . Go Bridal. It makes infinitely more sense to gradually introduce the kinds of measures you ideally would like in your life on an ongoing basis. (As opposed to embracing the latest No-Real-Food Macrobiotic Micromanaged Diet and All-Pain Microscopic-Gain Fitness Buster to overcomplicate your already complicated life.) Which isn't to say you're in the running for Narcissistic Bride of the Month if you work out with extra vigor or knock out the midmorning piece of chocoholic's delight. However it's wise to attempt to keep it all in perspective. Why, even consider applying that tiresome concept of "moderation." Remember, there's nothing more miserable than obsessive scale-watching. And there's nothing more pathetic than sitting like a poor puppy tableside with your tiny ration of boring, barely edible kibble, watching others chow down on real food.

THE FEARSOME FOUR

While there are many particulars (such as the Quest for Physical Perfection) that can cause you to Go Bridal, frequently triggers tend to fall into one of the following four camps: Family. Friends. Strangers. The Fiancé. And of course you, Ms. Bride, are potentially an active ingredient in any Going Bridal scenario. It takes two to tango, and the only thing more melodramatic than the tango is, after all, Going Bridal.

Read on, taking comfort perhaps. (You are definitely not alone!) Or heed the following as a collection of gentle warnings from women who have pranced down the bridal path and lived to tell the tale—along with a few brides currently in midprance—all of whom wish you the best of luck.

Do You Take This Family to Be Your Lawfully Wedded Family?

How many times have you heard someone say she wants to get married (at least in part) "for the family"? It gives one pause. Hmmm . . . What exactly does this person mean? After all, isn't marriage between you and one other person, that guy? Unless you are planning to re-create The Godfather or The Waltons (saints preserve us), chances are you're really doing this for yourself and your beloved, not for the clan.

That said, doubtless it is true that getting married will please some parents, grandparents, second cousins twice removed, your former stepfather's sister, and so on. The reality is that there are many people who place an extraordinary amount of faith in marriage as a way of validating a relationship. Or in the case of some parents, as an assurance that their kid is somehow now "taken care of" in the big picture of life.

On the one hand, this may be because the parents feel they can kick up their heels with relief that the fledgling is truly out of the nest, even if the fledgling is thirty-eight. But the parental relief factor isn't just about lessened responsibility, of course, it's about love. The infinitely repeated and infinitely complex "We just want you to be happy" mantra. It's about the idea that life will automatically be easier to navigate with love in your back pocket. Likely this is true, but as we all know (or should), marriage doesn't guarantee this will be the case from "I do" until "death do us." Still, for the close relatives of many a bride, marriage seems to signal a good chance that "our little Destiny" has met exactly that, her destiny, and no one has to be anxious about those creeps she used to date any more.

Family, ultimately and deep down (unless they truly are Cruel Evil Psycho-Family, in which case they're probably not coming to your wedding anyway), do want you to be happy. And yet all too frequently the pilot to a Going Bridal docudrama (or in some cases a Going Bridal epic trilogy) is all in the family.

A Word from the Bride About Family-Induced Going Bridal

What Evelyn Wanted: A simple, casual wedding.

What Evelyn Got: "Planning the wedding was like creating a magnification of issues with my family that I otherwise try to avoid or downplay. My mother and sisters had these conceptions of what I 'had' to do to plan my wedding. My mother, a sweetheart normally, is capable of a kind of quiet willfulness which she used to make sure I had the kind of wedding that conformed to her sense of what a wedding should be."

In the end Evelyn tried a compromise. She and her beau had a wedding day they wanted (intimate, outdoors, organized with friends), and then at a later date her family hosted a big party that was more to their taste. This proved a bit exhausting for Evelyn and beau, not to mention a tad annoying when inevitably some referred to the family party as "the wedding."

Evelyn Turns Back the Hands of Time: So what does Evelyn wish she'd done differently? Basically, she wishes she had put her foot firmly down, instead of doing the please-everyone dance. "I did try, but I wasn't firm enough. I genuinely wanted my family to be involved, but I couldn't reconcile that with having them follow my wishes."

What Jodi Wanted: A simple church wedding followed by a humongous party.

What Jodi Got: "Our families had many good ideas they were happy to share. A little too happy—they never stopped, they'd share their opinions over and over and over again. It was exhausting, it made our heads spin! At times people made us feel like if we didn't use their ideas, our wedding would be awful. In the end we had the church wedding and party, but after months of unnecessary hassles."

Jodi Turns Back the Hands of Time: "When people were sharing their ideas with us I wish I could have just told them, 'Thanks for the idea, but this is how we're going to do it.' End of story. If I could go back, I would be more assertive."

(Author's note: Evelyn and Jodi are currently considering a new joint business venture—Beleaguered Brides Assertiveness Training Seminars.)

What Andrea Wanted: To elope.

What Andrea Got: A big fat wedding. Why? Because she succumbed to the urge to "do it for the family." So even though she was living half a country away from the tribe, she and her mother planned the wedding by phone and fax, and the results were . . . not so great. "We quarreled constantly. In the end it made the wedding seem like more of a pain than a celebration. It did, unfortunately, dampen my enthusiasm for the whole thing. When I flew home and went to stay with Mom we had a huge fight and I ran out of the house. I stayed with my fiancé until the wedding, which was a drag because we thought since we were doing this for family anyway, we should do it the traditional way, and not see each other before the ceremony. It was all extremely tense."

Andrea Turns Back the Hands of Time: "I think the way you negotiate things with your family is probably the way you've always negotiated things with your family. I guess you could learn a whole new way of communicating with them, but that's a lot to ask during wedding planning. But it would have helped if I had thought in advance about where the problems would be, and had some suggestions or solutions. If I'd taken the time to do that I pretty much could have predicted what would make my mother nuts, and planned around it. I mean, I know the woman, after all! Either that or we really should have just eloped and lived with the consequences."

A Word from the Bride (in Progress)

What Jessica Wants: A beautiful traditional wedding, complete with the walk down the aisle in a puffy princessy dress on the arm of her dad.

What Jessica's Getting: "Things that are making me go mental during the planning are when I tell someone what I plan on doing for my wedding and they try and talk me out of it, or tell me what other options are out there. Just in case I didn't know. As if!"

Anti–Going Bridal Strategy: "When I start to feel annoyed I just say to myself, 'Opinions are like assholes, everybody has them,' and then just go on with my day."

(Author's note: Wow. You go, Jessica. Just remember not to say that out loud.)

What Felicia Wants: A wedding where her Italian family is comfortable with his Anglo family.

What Felicia's Getting: "Some of my relatives are very traditionally minded, very Catholic. They've already hinted, actually more than hinted, they will not come to a nondenominational wedding, which is what we're planning. This upsets my parents more than it bothers me, but their stress becomes our stress. Ultimately I know that the wedding will be fine, but it's too bad there will be a few people missing who could be there. On the other hand, maybe it's not—why should they be there if they feel so negative, who needs that!"

Anti–Going Bridal Strategy: "We're planning to have a bilingual wedding, so at least those older relatives who do come will be comfortable. As for the religion thing, we just keep saying, 'Sorry, but this is the way it has to be.' My mother's also taken to asking them, 'Which would you rather she has, an Anglican wedding or nondenominational?' That seems to help."

What Rena Wants: A wedding starring her family.

What Rena's Getting: "I always thought if I married I'd have my family in all the key roles. So my sister is my maid of honor. But she's driving me crazy! She has these Hollywood starlet mood swings, and seems to think that me asking her to be the maid of honor means our relationship as sisters should suddenly be on the therapist's couch. There's this constant analysis and scrutiny. I asked her because I thought it would be a celebration, and she's turning it into an inquisition."

Anti–Going Bridal Strategy: "I'm trying to get my nerve up to confront her—sit her down, ask her what's going on. Give her a chance to vent, and tell me what's really bugging her. I have a feeling some of her witchiness is because on some level she feels she's losing me, that I won't be in her life anymore. I'd rather we have a good cry than all this tension. And even though she's being kind of awful, I have to try and take the higher ground. Or else this could end up making the wedding day a living hell."

Anti–Going Bridal Warm-Ups

- Reread your notes from that assertiveness training course you took. (Alternatively, enroll in Assertiveness Training 101 ASAP.)
- Remove rose-colored glasses. (Translation: recall what your family is *really* like, and batten down the hatches.)
- "When you're smiling . . . the whole world smiles with you." (OK, so it doesn't, but it makes it harder for the whole world to pick on you if you stay positive.)

Friend (or Foe?)

Weddings, it does our feminist hearts no good to admit, can be a bit of a girly fest. They provide instant reasons for getting together for the most trivial of pursuits with our Best Girls. (Shopping! Debriefing cocktails! More shopping!) Weddings, as it does our feminist hearts even less good to admit, tend to focus to an absurd degree on The Bride. Consequently the bride needs help/advice/input/reassurance/support from her closest friends in order to deal with this unaccustomed spotlight. The intricacies of balancing friendships during wedding planning will be more fully explored in Chapter 4 ("Friends, Forever?"), but in the meantime, here are some all-too-typical scenarios to be on guard against, lest they induce as they did for these brides . . . Going Bridal.

Jamila's Chum, a.k.a. "I'll Do Anything for You": "This one friend told me that she really wanted to help. Desperately wanted to help. I believe her actual words were, 'I'll do anything for you.' So I asked her to go dress shopping with me. She stood me up. I asked her to look at flowers; she was so late the shop was closing. I asked her to meet me to talk about a prewedding chick night I wanted to have instead of a shower. She told me she really wanted to arrange a shower instead. I ended up agreeing. Then several people who came to the shower weren't even good friends of mine, they were friends of hers I wasn't that close to. But I should say in all fairness she did turn the shower into a helluva great party."

Friend or Foe?: In the actions–speak–louder–than–words camp, this one hangs in the balance.

Jamila Turns Back the Hands of Time: "When she first offered to help I should have asked her if she really had time. I knew she was crazy busy at work, but I didn't really bother investigating. I took her offer at face value. As for the no-show with dress shopping, I should have told her it really bugged me, which would have cleared the air. Instead I avoided her calls for a while. In truth, I still feel some resentment."

Lina's Chum, a.k.a. "But You Promised Me": Lina once told a friend that she would be one of her bridesmaids, should Lina ever get married. She was twenty-five at the time, and thought no more of it. It was in the category of Idle Bridal Chitchat. In fact, years later when she announced her plans to get married, she didn't even think of this woman. "She heard through another friend I was getting married. She called up and immediately asked me what I wanted the brides-maids to wear. I was so embarrassed I couldn't think of what to say to her. So I did the stupid thing and just said I'd have to let her know, instead of telling her the truth right away, which was that I wasn't planning to ask her to be a bridesmaid. It was awful. I completely freaked out about it, which drove my fiancé crazy."

Friend or Foe: "But You Promised Me" might have been a little shortsighted and/or desperate not to realize that Idle Bridal Chitchat is not the stuff of substance, especially several years after it flitted off into the ether, never to be mentioned again. Nonetheless, "But You Promised Me," however deluded, cannot be faulted for believing the promise.

Lina Turns Back the Hands of Time: "Finally I went to her and told her the truth. Of course I apologized profusely. But she was very hurt, and I completely understood why—I had been thoughtless, I admit it. Once a bit of time passed I talked to her about it again, and pointed out that the reason I hadn't planned to ask her was that we hadn't been close for a long time, although I still cared about her. But she still thought of us as close, that was the problem. Anyway, obvi-ously I never should have made that kind of casual statement if I didn't really mean it."

Michele's Chum, a.k.a. "Ms. Underwhelmed": "The most difficult response I got to my news I was getting married was from my best friend who I grew up with, who I always knew would be my maid of honor. I was so excited to tell her. I was at a mutual friend's house when my future maid of honor walked through the door. I just held out my hand. She took my hand, looked at the ring and looked up at me (and of course I had that face, the one where you look like you know you're going to be hugged really hard in a few seconds), and said, 'Oh.' Not, 'Ohhhhhhhhhh!!!' Just, 'Oh.' Then she proceeded to turn to our mutual friend and ask her if she was ready to go."

Friend or Foe: You're probably rooting "Foe! Foe!" but in fact, this typical Going Bridal–inciting scenario is complex. "Ms. Underwhelmed" certainly could and should have been more gracious, but she may well have had her own reasons for not going into ohmygawd mode. Possibly she had legitimate concerns about her friend's engagement. Or perhaps there were other, rather more significant things going on in her life at that moment that took emotional precedence. Maybe she was so overwhelmed with a sense of impending loss or change that she couldn't compose herself appropriately in the moment. Or could be she was a two-faced false friend from hell. The point is, it doesn't pay to jump to conclusions, a surefire cause of Going Bridal.

Michele Turns Back the Hands of Time: "I didn't deal well with that response, mostly because we were so close and in a million years I never, ever would have thought she would act like that. Honestly, the whole thing bummed me out so much that I didn't tell anyone else about the engagement for another week. Which actually for a soon-to-be bride is a long time! Her lack of excitement made me lose some of my excitement. But in the end I decided that I would trust that I did, in fact, know her well enough to realize she didn't mean anything by it. Now that I've been married for a little while and seen my other friends get engaged and plan their weddings I realize that no one else will ever care as much about the whole thing as you do. Sharing with friends and family does make it wonderful, but you can't orchestrate people's responses the way you can dictate what kind of hors d'oeuvres will be served. You need to move on!"

Beware Idle Bridal Chitchat

- Running into someone and saying "Oh, you should come to my wedding," and not really meaning it is *not* the same thing as saying "Let's do lunch, dahling," with a totally insincere air kiss (off).
- Agreeing to have your fiancé's best buddies from out of town stay at your apartment in the week leading up to the wedding but secretly scheming to get them into a motel at the last minute is at best foolish.
- Telling your girlfriends you want them all to be equally involved in your wedding when there is only one chick you plan to have standing at your side on The Day will come back to bite you on your bridal butt.

Complete Strangers Are Ruining My Life

Fear and loathing of the unknown is a theme song for some women who Go Bridal. Closely aligned to paranoia, the idea that strangers are out to get you can become an all-too-common feature in the lives of many brides. Somewhat understandably, given that planning a wedding can require the input, expertise, and skills of a fleet of people you barely know. Consequently there are bound to be unexpected wrinkles, perhaps even heaving mountains, in the canvas that is your wedding-to-be, callously created, so you feel, by these evil-doers. All it seems to take for some brides is an ill-placed word from one of these strangers to tarnish their bridal queendom. Here are a few modern-day fairy tales from brides who found that dealing with the unknown made them . . . Go Bridal.

Andrea and the Big Bad DJ: Andrea is a musician, and she had specific ideas about what kind of music she wanted at her wedding. She and her fiancé would have liked a live band, but since there wasn't the budget they hired a DJ. "I thought I gave this guy a fairly clear idea of the kind of music I wanted played, and asked him to give me a playlist. This was about two months before the wedding. About two weeks before the wedding I finally saw this playlist, which had some songs I wouldn't play at an enemy's funeral. Can we just say one word: 'Feelings'? I freaked!" What happened next was, oh, not so nice. Andrea's mother, with whom she was organizing the wedding long-distance, decided to give the DJ a talking-to. The DJ, who had not had any previous follow-up calls from mother or child, walked. Andrea blamed her mother, because she thought her mom should have found a way to tactfully negotiate. Her mother blamed her because she was only voicing what Andrea, hysterical down the long-distance line, had said. And we can only presume the DJ, despite possibly being unable to pay his rent that month, was at least hugely relieved not to have to deal with these women who were . . . Going Bridal.

The Moral of the Story: "I should have made sure I got the playlist earlier, or I should have given him specific song titles and artists. I shouldn't have just relied on this complete stranger without some serious consultation."

Lina and the Wicked Boss: Lina's boss's boss, with whom she had only a nodding acquaintance, stopped her in the hall at work to wish her well upon hearing of her upcoming wedding. Lina thought this was charming. Until her boss told her that this selfsame man had mentioned he would prefer the company not "do" anything on company premises to celebrate personal matters. And that the company, as delighted as it was that one of its flock should be getting married, would certainly not put its money where its mouth was and pony up for any related fete. This was problematic, given that Lina's colleagues, a friendly but not terribly prosperous bunch, had already planned to use the lunchroom/lounge for a small celebration, catering some simple treats on their departmental budget. Lina's boss was apologetic, but what could she do? Lina's colleagues took her out for a drink instead, but then there were grumblings about the place that was chosen, where the average price of a glass of wine was some people's entertainment budget for the weekend.

The Moral of the Story: "The guy was a jerk, although totally within his rights, of course. But when I knew the original plan had been scuppered, I should have said to everyone, 'Look, let's just go someplace cheap,' rather than ending up in this expensive lounge. Because what happened was some people drank a lot, some people barely had anything, and it was all on one bill. So even though it was supposed to be for me, I chipped in a lot of money for the bill since I knew not everyone could afford it."

Jamila and the Ice Maiden: Jamila had been recommended a designer who was known to be somewhat "difficult," but whose work was fabulous, producing just the kind of knockout frock Jamila envisioned herself wearing on The Day. Jamila trotted off to the haughty designer's boutique, and happily introduced herself to the genius in question. She was met with a curt, "You need to make an appointment," and was completely ignored for the next twenty minutes she spent window-shopping. During this time said designer attended to the wants of a customer who came in after Jamila, but was obviously "from money" and managed to get friendly service sans appointment. Jamila then booked an appointment, the first of far too many, and spent months kowtowing to this woman who was at best civil, at worst disrespectful.

The Moral of the Story: "I really wish I'd just walked away the first time she was rude. I mean, yes, the dress was beautiful, but I can never look at it without thinking of those torturous fittings and unpleasant times I spent waiting to talk to her. The people you surround yourself with during wedding planning really can have an impact on your state of mind. She just about ruined things for me."

Never Assume—It Makes an Ass out of U and Me

- Assuming that just because you left a message with a _____ (fill in the blank: catering company, dressmaker, florist), the vendor will call you back within a reasonable amount of time, is like assuming the guy you shagged once after a debauched party would call you, ever.

- Assuming the bartender at your after-work local is going to say, "Drinks on the house!" when she hears the news of your impending nuptials is like assuming you will fork over thirty bucks for a baby shower present for whatsherface in HR.

- Assuming that your amiable local florist will cheerfully accept your announcement that dried cattails from the local slough will take the place of any store-bought posies on your wedding day is like assuming your hairdresser will jump for joy at your decision to do your own cut . . . and color.

The Other Half

This book, and the average wedding, is unabashedly bride-centric. Which isn't to say that the groom should be totally ignored. (Why, there is an entire chapter devoted to him toward the end of the book, called "Oh Yeah, Whatshisname.") But in the initial list of categories of triggers causing Going Bridal (a.k.a. The Fearsome Four), it has to be said that the groom can be, like it or not, one of the primary catalysts to the condition. To get a preliminary analysis of how this (dys)functions, let's turn to another "word from the bride."

She Says, She Says

Share the Load Versus Spoil the, Um, Child: Karen was forty-five and her husband was in his fifties when they got engaged. Both had been married before. When they began planning their wedding, Karen was shocked by her intended's assumption that she would take on the lioness's share of the grunt work. (Which consequently became growl work, as she found herself snarling at him to carry his weight.) "Eventually I realized that he just assumed that as a woman I would want to take over most of the planning. It turned out that his first wife had done just that, so there was a precedent set. Which isn't to say he should have assumed I would be like her—after all, part of his attraction to me is based on how different I am! My reaction to his lack of input went from hurt to annoyance to a sense almost of betrayal. After all, we were a team, and his seeming indifference to planning our wedding made me feel like he was letting us down."

Karen Turns Back the Hands of Time: "I wish I had done what I eventually did, but right at the beginning of the process. Which was to talk about our expectations of how the wedding planning would go. I mean, I assumed we'd share everything equally. Part of the point for me of having a wedding, after having been married before when I was so much younger, was that I didn't want it to be conventional. And I didn't want to fall into that stereotypical thing where the woman takes over and the guy just nods, "Uh-huh, whatever you say, dear." I assumed he felt the same way."

My Way Is the Right Way: Lynn is a self-described control freak. She genuinely believes that in most instances she knows the best way to do certain kinds of things—pretty much anything to do with matters of a practical sort. Problem was, her fiancé, who had to date tolerated that aspect of her personality, pitched a fit. "The wedding planning was insane. He'd question every decision I'd make, and accused me of being obsessed with the wedding at the expense of our relationship."

Lynn Turns Back the Hands of Time: "The smartest thing we did was to take time out. Not of the relationship—but from the planning. We went away for a long weekend, spent the first part just hanging out, and then finally started talking about why things had gotten so out of hand. He admitted his scrutiny of my decisions was based in part on his own fears that I wasn't as committed to the relationship, to the idea of marriage, as he was. And I admitted part of my desire to control the planning was that it was a way of controlling my anxieties about this huge step we were taking. And also that I really do think I have a better sense of how to manage details. You can imagine how fun a conversation that was! But actually it did help—and he even acknowledged that I am better with details, primarily because they matter to me more than they do to him. Still, I wish I'd lightened up—looking back I can see I really was unnecessarily obsessive."

How Much Is That Wedding in the Window?: Jacquie was plagued by money issues throughout the wedding planning—and according to her, most of the issues stemmed from her beloved groom-to-be. "We drew up a budget for the wedding, but inevitably it started to creep over the amount we had agreed on. Whenever that would happen he'd start doing backflips, make these irrational statements like, "I guess that means we'll just have to cancel then," things like that. After we'd already put down deposits for a hall and a caterer, so it really didn't make any sense at all. And of course on an emotional level it just sent me over the brink. 'What, so you *don't* want to get married now?'"

Jacquie Turns Back the Hands of Time: "I admit I didn't handle what I saw as his irrational responses to money issues very well. I could have been more empathetic, given it was my money too, but instead I tended just to get angry with him, and tell him he was behaving like a child. And we all know how much people like being told that! Pretty much every time he'd flip out I'd get angry or act hurt, instead of trying to talk it through. Finally we had such a meltdown we did end up talking it through, and came to some agreements about how we'd manage the overspending, and how we'd talk to one another about it. I think we could have got to that point a lot sooner, though, if we'd both acted more maturely."

A PARTING THOUGHT

You and your betrothed are a team, and whether that is an Olympic-level baton relay with a handoff imbued with grace and style, or a three-legged race where you awkwardly lurch together across the finish line, will be up to the two of you.

But gentle reader, fear not. While, as we have seen, Going Bridal is a genuine concern, the condition is certainly quite manageable. And perhaps in its very management, there is a lesson to be learned. Cast your mind ahead into the future, where you and the Hub are a-settin' and a-rockin'. Which would you rather look back on? A marriage where full-scale Going Bridal was the blueprint, followed by many reenactments over the years, or a marriage where some of the skills and qualities developed during wedding planning set the stage for a lifetime of good communication? A lifetime of being together, not as one, but as two, devoted to the idea of one good marriage.

2

The Answer's Yes!

A Tale of a Former Holdout . . . a.k.a. The Bride

When I woke up today my first thought after "Must . . . have . . . coffee" was, "Wait a minute, something's different this morning."

Sleep suddenly vanished.

"Hey! We decided to get married last night!"

This revelation was immediately followed by a wave of completely idiotic blissful happiness.

"I'm going to be a bride." I murmured it out loud just to give it a whirl, and it sounded so absurd I started laughing. This had absolutely no impact on my fiancé ("fiancé," now that's even *more* bizarre), who was slumbering beside me in his usual inimitable style. Nothing wakes him up short of direct action, so I spoke loudly into one ear.

"We're getting married! Isn't it great, but kind of . . . weird?"

He surfaced just enough to mumble, "Why is it weird?" then rolled over into a more profound level of sleep.

After the first cuppa joe I considered the question. It's weird because I've never imagined having a wedding, let alone daydreamed about princess-cut diamonds or what have you—the wedding paraphernalia that some I could name seem to have known about since birth. I never saw myself having anything in my life people could refer to as The Big Day. In fact, I've never even fantasized about being married, period. A lasting relationship, yes. A Mrs. degree, no.

To date I haven't achieved either. True, I've lived with a guy before, and my fiancé (will I ever be able to call him that with a straight face?) and I have been sharing an apartment for months now. Long enough that we could just say we're heading down the virtual aisle to a common-law marriage.

For some reason neither of us wants that, though. (Among the more trivial because it sounds so, well, "common.") And it's not like I need the proverbial "piece of paper" to feel more committed, or a wedding extravaganza to dazzle my parents' friends. (Given half of them "live in sin" anyway.) No, as hopelessly corny and clichéd as it may be, it's more about telling the world (or at least the people I know and love in it) how committed I am. And more important, I want him to know, to *really* know how strongly I feel about our relationship. Oh, I suppose I might as well admit it, it's also about differentiating between my, ahem, fiancé and what my sister calls, to his face no less, his "predecessors." Yes indeedy, he really is the man for me.

I'm pleased to report that when he proposed there wasn't a second's hesitation before I said, "Yes." Mind you, there was an instant afterward where I wouldn't have objected to a reenactment. I mean, "Yes" is a little underwhelming as a response. Still, there was much toasting and hand-holding and waiters congratulating, which made it a fantastic, blurry happy night.

But this morning in the cold light of day (actually it was rather warm, which made me start musing about the possibilities of an outdoor wedding), the "W" words loomed large. Words like, gulp, *wife.* Totally foreign territory. But I figure it'll be like traveling, the unknown is half the fun.

Fortunately my friends and family adore my betrothed. (Tee hee.) I'm sure they'll think marrying him is the best decision I've made since realizing a career as a vet really was impractical for someone allergic to fur-bearers. They may be a little taken aback, what with my track record and all (and certain friends will no doubt rag me about my defection from the "wedding holdout" camp), but I see much gleeful champagne toasting in my immediate future.

My husband-to-be was still slumbering.

"If you're going to sleep all morning I think I'll call the family. And Edie. And Angela. And Priya. And maybe just one or two other people," I announced.

"Mmm," he murmured, "Nice idea."

The Mom et al. were thrilled. As were Edie and co., although they insist I'm going to get as loopy as they are now that I'm engaged too. (Never!) But imagine my surprise when one of my other friends said, and I quote, "You're going to do what? But why?"

You're Going to Do What?

Why get married? A question that was probably once about as common as "Why have 2.5 children and the picket fence?" In other words, in the not-too-distant past it was the mirror version of the question that stared determined singletons in the face—Why *not* get married? But the times they have a-changed. No doubt in large part due to such things as the so-called sexual revolution of the 1960s and all that followed.

These days, the "over half of all marriages end in divorce" stat is regularly rolled out like some evil carpet, daring us to defy it, to walk down it toward the altar of supposed doom.

And we do. In the United States alone, 2.4 million weddings occur each year; in Canada, over 150,000. By the age of thirty, *three-quarters* of the female population of the United States has been married. Naturally enough (or for those who buy into conspiracy theories about the profiteering ways of big business, "unnaturally enough"), there is a huge industry related to weddings. Reportedly $72 billion is spent on weddings each year in the United States. Aside from the costs of caterers, tuxedos, or the Royal Doulton, the industry surrounding wedding planning is stunning in its relentless efforts to attract our attention. Think of the staggering weight (and equivalent costs) of bridal magazines, the convention center floors swarmed by purveyors of wedding-related frippery, the bridal boutiques that rival paint stores with their imagined shades of white.

Then there's the fascination with others getting hitched, which never seems to wane. (How many people surreptitiously skip from the front section of the Sunday *New York Times* to read the jaw-dropping "vows" way back in the weddings pages, for example? More than will admit, you can be sure.) This gawking at weddings is not-so-subtly encouraged by the most pervasive (or should that be invasive) medium available—television. Reality TV brought us endless rounds of shows where the ultimate goal was that two people would—at some point following a hideously humiliating elimination process—gallop down the bridal path. Celebrities allow their weddings to be filmed, and then graciously agree to have choice segments broadcast around the world. Joe Couple can also tell their real-life wedding story to TV cameras, clearly refusing to believe that there really is such a thing as "too much information."

Finding "true love" on the tube in front of millions of strangers is only one offshoot of wedding obsession. Some see the wedding itself as more of a lavish production than a private ceremony, whether it takes place at a tried-and-true locale (a church, your living room) or someplace more exotic (the end of a bungee cord, the First Church of the Elvis Impersonator). You can even get hitched in cyberspace. (It's virtually if not legally binding.) And of course you can create a wedding website of your own, providing you really believe folks hunger to read about your innovative Native American/Celtic ceremony followed by step-dancing around the traditional venison and haggis barbeque. Some couples get so plumb worked up at the notion of publicly displaying their nuptials and the surrounding festivities that they even get married more than once. (So as to have something with which to update their website, one supposes.) For instance, the couple who married each other three times, claiming, "We're so married we can't get divorced!" (Actually, they could, but no sense distracting them from planning wedding number four.)

Fictional accounts are as thick as June weddings—there's no end to wedding-themed books and movies. It shouldn't come as a surprise that *My Big Fat Greek Wedding* became the biggest-grossing independent film to date when it came out in 2002, a movie that the public adored, but critics lambasted for its reliance on stereotypes about ethnicity, families, and weddings. Ah, but those stereotypes come from the same place many of us do—where the repetitive machinations of our families makes us laugh or weep, depending on our mood. And since the inherent wackiness of families is displayed at its finest (or worst, depending on your point of view) through the rituals marking rites of passage, by definition families and weddings with their supposed stereotypes are entertaining, whether big, fat, and Greek or short, slim, and Canadian (see author bio).

The silver screen aside, it's particularly fascinating that many of us still want to marry given twenty-first century realities. After all, excepting couples from specific backgrounds (cultural, religious, or merely idiosyncratic) where their families will do their utmost to make the lives of the couple living together a living hell, there is nothing to stop anyone from merely shacking up. There's also nothing to prevent a couple from sharing their lives but maintaining separate residences. Or, should a person choose to do so, she or he can have multiple partners of either sex. Another option is eschewing a romantic or sexual relationship altogether. It's the era of anything goes, and we're not talkin' "a glimpse of stocking." We're talking full range of choice.

And yet, and yet . . . those statistics (2.4 *million* weddings a year in the United States!) stare us down, proving incontrovertibly that many of us still want to take the great leap into the unknown abyss of "officially" committing to one other person—marriage. And more often than not, we want it preceded by some kind of ceremony called a wedding.

Why Wed?

The question remains, why wed? Here's some fun (and not so fun) speculation from a group of university students of both sexes who believe you might want to get married for any of the following reasons: To have sex. To avoid loneliness. To bear children. As a way of altering "the boredom of dating for years." To be like everyone else. To get a joint bank account. To get "a fancy ring." To share everything with another person. To get out of "a hectic lifestyle" and enter into "an organized environment."

Most depressing on their long list was the sad comment, "Because you will get half of everything if you get divorced." Most uplifting: "Because of a deep love."

This final notion is substantiated by thirty-eight-year-old Jen, who believed for the longest time that she wasn't "the shacking up" let alone "the marrying" kind. Then along came Adam.

"I never considered a truly serious commitment with any of the men I went out with through my twenties and early thirties. I just didn't see myself as being the type to settle down. But it was completely different with Adam. So much so that actually I proposed to him! There was just a quality of maturity in our relationship that I felt wasn't there in previous relationships. We wanted the same kinds of things in life, we had a shared vision of a lifestyle together, of a way of being in the world as a couple. Our values were fundamentally similar. The timing finally felt right. And ultimately I knew the love I felt for Adam was just much, much deeper than anything I'd experienced before."

The extensive Going Bridal research team discovered that Jen's Short List of Reasons to Marry This One is not an uncommon phenomenon. For many women the decision to marry is based on a combo deal, multiple reasons that somehow dovetail nicely. If, for example, marrying someone is what you truly want to do and it just so happens that it will also make your parents get down on their knees and sing hallelujah, well praises be. Even better if it means you can move out of that basement bachelorette pad smelling of old ferret. But it's nice to know that the pragmatic reasons flow from something that is essentially more profound.

Take Hannah, for instance. She's a successful, feisty New Yorker who never thought she would get married, but then had a change of heart after a long-distance relationship with Dave, a Torontonian.

"On a practical level Dave and I had no choice but to get married so that we could live together in the same country. Getting married was merely step one in the green-card process. On a more personal level, I simply wanted to marry Dave. We fit so well together and getting married seemed like the natural next step in our relationship."

For Hannah, the decision to marry was made after countless hours in airport lounges provided her with ample opportunity to consider her choice. Obviously not everyone decides to marry after such extensive pondering. (Talk show TV wouldn't exist were that the case.) No, frequently the decision to marry is a tad more haphazard, springing primarily from an emotional impulse. (Ideally followed by a deeper scrutiny of one's motives.) This was the situation for Mary.

"When we first decided to get married I honestly don't think either of us understood why we felt compelled to do so. We eventually admitted this to each other, which was kind of scary. But fortunately after a marriage preparation course and conversations with our priest and other married couples, we did agree that marriage really was a satisfying way to affirm our love and commitment to each other, and a way to celebrate that with family."

Mary and her husband planned to wed in a Catholic church, and one of the requirements to do so was the marriage prep course. At first they were a little skeptical, thinking that as young urban sophisticates the church-designed course might prove, well, somewhat old-fashioned. Instead they were pleasantly surprised to find that it offered them a "guided period of reflection," ultimately helping them to feel confident about their choice to wed. But what about people who don't come hardwired with religious traditions: how do they fare after saying yes? Evelyn, a bride who confesses to having been "ambivalent to negative about the idea of marriage," puts it this way.

"I think it's the biggest leap of faith I ever made. There were no tests we could take, nothing to confirm whether we were making the right choice. But getting married for me was more about choosing a path of love and positivity. It stands in opposition to so much doubt and worry and cynicism in the world. Getting married also felt like an official starting line to another level of our lives together."

The idea of marriage as a passage into something deeper is clearly a concept that entices many twenty-first century couples to tie the knot. It's a voyage that isn't charted by some predetermined timeline—long gone are the days of practically mandatory weddings by the age of twenty-five. (Amen, sister!) Annie, a forty-nine-year-old woman who lived together with her man for nine years before saying "I do" saw getting married as icing on an already quite delicious cake.

Musings On Marrying

"Rituals are important. Nowadays it's hip not to be married. I'm not interested in being hip."
—JOHN LENNON

"Women who marry early are often overly enamored of the kind of man who looks great in wedding pictures and passes the maid of honor his telephone number."
—ANNA QUINDLEN

"I love being married. It's so great to find one special person you want to annoy for the rest of your life."
—RITA RUDNER

"Marriage, to women as to men, must be a luxury, not a necessity; an incident of life, not all of it."
—SUSAN B. ANTHONY

"She's got gaps, I got gaps. Together we fill gaps."
—ROCKY

"The men that women marry, and why they marry them, will always be a marvel and a mystery to the world."
—HENRY WADSWORTH LONGFELLOW

"Marriage is our last, best chance to grow up."
—JOSEPH BARTH

Three Possibly Good Reasons to Decide to Marry

1. Love. (If you have to ask if "love" is really what you're feeling, maybe consider dating the guy a little longer.)
2. The old "outward symbol of inner commitment." Social conditioning or not, this concept feels real enough to shape the lives of many happily marrieds.
3. To celebrate the bond you already have with your intended with the community that forms your world, a.k.a. friends and family (and inevitably a few strangers).

Three Probably Suspect Reasons to Decide to Marry

1. Because you spend so much time at his place anyway, and ferrying that toothbrush back and forth is getting ever so tiresome.
2. Because you get along pretty well, at least much of the time. Besides, calling him your "partner" makes you shudder.
3. Because he indicates he wants to be a citizen of your country and you think, "What the hey, he really is a lovely guy. So what if we don't speak the same language?"

Three Decidedly Moronic Reasons to Decide to Marry

1. Because you loathe dating almost as much as you dislike your maiden name.
2. Because you think no one better will come along.
3. Because it sure will reduce those mortgage payments.

"The idea was, 'Hey, we're really already married so let's celebrate it and make it official!' And there is something very nice about being officially married. A feeling of commitment and contentment." Annie also had emotional and psychological considerations connected to her extended-blended family. "Being a wife rather than a girlfriend seems to make me a real stepmother, a real stepgrandma . . ." All a far cry from the reasons she cites for her first marriage at age twenty. "Then I got married as a sort of 'I'm-twenty-now' reflex. He asked, and I thought, 'Why not? OK.'"

Probably not the best reason to take such a giant emotional and legal step, but we'll forgive Annie given her tender age at the time. Still, if you're on the cusp of making the commitment, you may want to heed Annie's example and consider introducing an element of rationality into something that admittedly isn't an entirely rational decision. (Saying you'll attach yourself to one other foible-encrusted person for the rest of your life? Um, does that make sense on paper?) So if you're still just considering the idea, or have decided to marry but are feeling a trifle shaky, you might want to actually articulate your reasons for marrying this particular person. Perhaps even write down your motives for considering such a life-altering choice. Mull them over. Meditate upon them. Recalling that if the intent really is "the long term," as in (drum roll) The Rest of Your Life, it would be wise to take the decision rather seriously. It's possible if more people took the time to evaluate their choice then maybe, just maybe, those divorce stats would shrink.

Which isn't to say that it would stop women from . . . Going Bridal.

The Case of State, Church, Family . . . Versus Me and Him

So what do you say when you give someone the news and the person's oh-so-sensitive response is, "Why do you want to get married?" Depending on the nature of your relationship with that person you may have any number of possible comebacks. (Although "It's none of your business" rarely works well, even when delivered with a smile.) You could, of course, articulate your reasons in obsessive detail, which may well bore the other person so much that he or she never wants to talk to you about your wedding or anything else ever again. On the other hand, if the person asks out of loving curiosity he or she may be riveted to your every innermost thought and feeling, to the point where even you are sick of talking about it. Worst-case scenario is if you suspect that underlying the question "Why wed?" there's a thinly veiled sneer. You sense there is a suggestion being advanced that the only reason you are getting married is because you are so conditioned, so ground down by social norms and centuries-old tradition that you have become merely another lamb to the slaughter of marriage. In this event, you may want to be prepared. One way of doing that is by knowing something of the history of Western white weddings and by understanding that in most instances you are participating in traditions that were formed to a significant degree by patriarchs, priests, and politicians. Then at the very least you can knowledgeably say things like, "Why yes, I am thrilled that our wedding cake is a symbol of breaking bread over the bride's head to celebrate her fertility. It's a pre–seventeenth century tradition that's fab but a trifle messy. And after all, we are planning to have kids."

Entire books have been written about various aspects of wedding history, and you may want to seek them out. But likely not, so try this condensed version. Think of it as a sort of trailer to a millennium's worth of feature films devoted to the Western so-called "white wedding" tradition.

Wedding History in Four Paragraphs or Less: In the beginning, there were tribes. No weddings needed. Then the notion of pairing up started seeming more desirable. The first marriages were apparently a little sudden. The groom and his warrior buddies (best men by any other name) would slip into an enemy tribe's camp and kidnap a bride. In some sectors there was the equally charming notion of purchasing a bride. Which probably gave us the word *wedding*, from the Anglo-Saxon word *wedd*, which, sad to say, means "to wager or gamble."

In pre-Christian Europe, weddings were all in the family—fathers and families largely dictated what was what. Then the church got involved sometime around the eleventh century, with the Roman Catholic Church taking away the parental right to sanction marriage. (Although it was still several centuries before you had to actually get married *in* a church.) Along came King Henry VIII a few hundred years later, who for some strange reason wanted jurisdiction over marriage . . . and divorce. (Think Anne Boleyn.) To get his previous marriage annulled to marry Anne, he wrested control over the English church and thereby paved the way for state control over weddings.

If you want to dig into the reasons why family, church, and the state have battled for this ownership of weddings, you'll find yourself tunneling through a labyrinth of issues, a twisty trail of religious beliefs, social beliefs, political power struggles, and economics. But you probably don't want to do that, you merely want to refute those cynical antiwedding naysayers.

So what about all the myriad of traditions we're told we "buy into" once we decide to get married? There are many and conflicting versions as to the origins of what some call "the customary elements" of a Western wedding. But here are a few generally held beliefs you might want to think upon. Of course ultimately whatever you decide to include in your wedding is what you and your betrothed are comfortable with, regardless of its origin.

Symbols: Love 'Em or Leave 'Em

- *White.* Wear it and recall that in the 1500s it symbolized virginity. Or recall that white looks great on you and since you don't play tennis it's probably your only opportunity. Or ditch it entirely and wear red because white makes you look like hell on a hangover.

- *Dressing bridesmaids and ushers identically.* At one time brides-maids and ushers wore the same getup as the bride and groom—apparently so that in the event that a spurned suitor turned up at the wedding, he or she would be confused as to the identity of the actual bride or groom, and thus be less able to disrupt the proceedings. (Makes you wonder how close a relationship the spurned had with the spurnee, doesn't it?) Other versions suggest the matching clothes were for protec-tion against evil spirits, and you know how easily confused they are. Recall this tradition and realize that old flames and evil spirits are no excuse for dressing a group of your dearest girlfriends in seafoam green.

- *The standardized white wedding.* The bride in frothy white, the attendants in matching duds, the shower(s), the stag, the DJ, the matching-everything, the honeymoon, and so on and so forth are (yup, afraid so) strongly linked to capitalism. Wed-dings were often small and impromptu in North America until the nineteenth century, when retailers had their "eureka" moment. Things really heated up when *Bride's Magazine* was founded in 1934, creating a national advertising vehicle in the United States. For some brides nowadays this looks like mon-eygrubbing, and it serves as motivation to have as simple and homemade a wedding as possible. Of course, if your cousin owns a bridal boutique you may feel differently.

- *The processional.* You know, the bit where you walk down an aisle with a dad? It's historically a symbol of the bride moving from one locale to another, from one sort of status to a differ-ent sort. Oh all right, stop mincing words—it's being "given away"! But should you choose to observe this tradition you may prefer to see it as a symbol of your love for your father. If so, more power to you.

- *Kissing the bride and exchanging rings.* These are pre-Christian traditions: among other things, they suggest that words are not enough to bind our physical selves to each other. Got a problem with that? Find me a person without symbols or rituals in her or his life, and you will find me one dud spud.

- *Bouquet carrying.* Consider carrying a gathering of garlic and herbs to ward away the evil spirits. These bouquets were the predecessor of flowers, which can symbolize both fertility and eternal love. Or carry nothing, but try not to wring your hands and scrunch up your skirt.

- *Stag or bachelor parties.* These began with the ancient Spartans, known for their nice traditions. (Abandoning less-than-perfect babies on hillsides, for example.) Spartan soldiers would get together the night before the wedding to do some of the same things some twenty-first century men get together to do before their weddings. Only the Spartans took the "bye-bye to bachelorhood" one step further and swore allegiance to their comrades in arms. (Hey, who's marrying who?) All to say, this is why for many more enlightened grooms the word "stag" is verboten. Try "boys' night out" or "gentlemen's soiree" instead.

- *The something old, something new jingle.* A Victorian invention. "Something old" was to ensure your ancestors' blessing on your union. "Something new" refers to a boatload of ideas, including such lovely notions as the wearing of someone else's dress might bring you bad luck. Which seems in direct contradiction to the "something borrowed." Mind you, if the borrowed item was from a happily married woman it was supposed to ensure the bride's happiness. As for the "blue," that originates in the prewhite era when blue, not white, symbolized purity. (Easier to launder, too bad it fell out of fashion.)

And the last line of the little ditty, "a silver sixpence in her shoe," which is less familiar these days, was code for emotional and financial prosperity. (What's more uncomfortable than wearing a veil? Try a sixpence in your shoe.) Perhaps you don't want to celebrate like the Victorians. You could try "Something new, something new, something new, something new," which seems to serve many brides very well.

DIAGNOSING SAYING-YES GOING BRIDAL: THE SYMPTOMS, THE TRIGGERS, THE TREATMENTS, THE GOALS

So the answer is yes! Hopefully you're feeling pretty spectacular about the decision. (It *is* a decision, right, not a whim of the moment?) But you may find once you announce your plans a number of issues surface, issues that could cause you to exhibit early symptoms of Going Bridal. Some of these concerns may become triggers closely aligned with those diagnosed in Chapter 3, "But I Love My Family, Really, I Do." Still, there are certain matters that can be seen as discreet entities relating to the postannouncement phase, best dealt with independently.

Symptoms of Saying-Yes Going Bridal

- You tell a colleague you've just said yes, and when she says "That's nice" and changes the subject you leave her office inwardly fuming about her lack of interest in what is, after all, headline news.
- A relative asks you why you haven't set the date yet and you snap, "What's the big deal with this date-setting thing anyway!"

- A stranger at a party wonders why you've decided to get married when you already live with your partner; you roll your eyes and look for another drink.
- Upon hearing the news one of your friends whines, "But I always thought I'd be married by now. It's just not fair," and you find yourself grinding your teeth.

Trigger: Why Wasn't I the First to Know?

The day after Maria and her beau decided to get married she spent from morning to nightfall on the phone, interrupted only by forays to relatives' houses to share the moment. Her clan is pretty trad, and she knew they'd all want to hear the news and celebrate ASAP. The next day her sister bumped into one of Maria's more casual friends who hadn't yet heard the joyous tidings. Next thing Maria knew this friend was on the horn bleating about how terrible it was to hear about the engagement secondhand. Maria didn't cope with that so well. "I was too exhausted from all that racing around to even think of what to say to her. And I was getting really tired of not having any time with my fiancé to just enjoy the early stages of being engaged. I didn't want to spend every waking second on the phone or drinking another glass of homemade wine in someone's living room."

This trigger is an annoyance that one could well do without. You call _____ (fill in the blank: Poor Old Dad, former best friend Destiny, the boyfriend you once almost married) and tell them your news. Their response, after the initial congratulations (one hopes they at least get that far), is delivered in a tone of "You told so-and-so before me? How could you?" They moan, "I can't believe you didn't tell me before you told _____ (fill in the blank: your mother, your best friend for all time, your neighbor who eavesdropped on the proposal).

The Treatment: Swallow It

The Goal: To save your strength for more intense triggers to Going Bridal that are lurking in the wings.

The Application: There is nothing you can do to truly mollify the feelings of someone who feels she or he wasn't told your news at the appropriate time. This is because there really is no appropriate time. (Those who believe etiquette is handed down from time immemorial are those who will not read this book.) Think about it, what woman in the first flush of postengagement excitement creates a flow chart to determine exactly who will be told when and why? (OK, don't answer that question, no doubt she exists.) All you can do is tell the aggrieved party you had scads of people to tell and you didn't map it out in advance. That the extreme closeness you feel with said party is still unrivalled by any other, and the order of "the telling" is no indication of anything of consequence.

On the other hand, if there is a reason you didn't tell Indignant Friend or Relative first (for example, you knew she would immediately want to start talking florists), you have a few options. You could tell her of course it is incredibly important to you to share this news with her, but you wanted to do so when you were ready to start talking florists. (Although if you know you'll never want to talk florists with her, this is a losing proposition.) Or, as is often the case with imparting such news, you wanted to do it in person rather than over the phone. And that means having to line up all your social ducks for the weeks ahead to facilitate the firsthand telling, which just plain takes time.

Another likely (and honest) scenario you can unveil is that you wanted to tell your parents and sibs first, given they are immediate family and all. Failing the relevance or efficacy of any of the above, you move to your final option. Simply apologize. As in, "I am very sorry I hurt your feelings." Either way, you pretty much just have to swallow it.

Who Ya Gonna Tell? Top Five Oddball Announcements

Sometimes there is a delirious rush of energy after getting engaged, and a bride finds herself telling anyone and everyone, for instance:

1. A complete stranger on the street. This can be a thrill—especially when you get the "Oh-isn't-that-fantastic-how-lovely-good-for-you-dear" response.

2. A local merchant, who then turns around and tells everyone in the shop his favorite customer (suddenly you have achieved that status) is getting married, and the whole place turns into a mini–engagement party.

3. Someone at work you've never gotten along with, and instead of the usual squaring off over who gets bigger billing with The Boss, you find yourself having a deeply engrossing conversation about the best place to shop for wedding shoes.

4. A little kid who looks up at you and says, "What's 'getting married' mean?"

5. The incredibly taciturn security guy at your building, who actually cracks a smile and says, "Congratulations."

The Trigger: He's Not the Man I Hoped for You

This trigger to Going Bridal can be a bit of a shocker, as Michele discovered. "I was in the car driving with my aunt and out of the blue she said, 'I don't really like him for you. Never thought you'd actually marry him.' I remember being speechless and decided not to say anything."

Michele's choice not to dignify this with a reply is understandable. (For one thing, who wants to drive off the road when there's a wedding to plan?) Some of us are lucky gals and our friends and families think our chosen consort is the one they would have selected for us had they been invited to do so. But sometimes friends or relatives enter into the "I know what's best for you" stakes, for some reason forgetting that this never actually pays off.

Think back, for example, to your college days when some well-meaning older relative said your career choice of forensic science instead of computer data entry was foolish. Did that make you smack your forehead, exclaiming, "Of course, why did I spend the last three years staying up late to read *Crime Scene Investigation Monthly* when I could have been learning to type?" It did not. The same dynamics apply to choosing a partner and to the reaction others have to your choice. True, if you are in a situation that is in some way abusive you may, in the depths of despair, actually listen to the advice of the friend telling you to lose the creep. But short of that, you make your proverbial bed yourself, and you lie in it. (Hopefully not with the proverbial dog with fleas.) It's no wonder someone telling you your choice is wrong or misguided can be one mighty trigger to . . . Going Bridal.

The Treatment: Confirm or Deny

The Goal: So that the situation doesn't escalate to the point where the person with "issues" about your choice refuses to come to the wedding, or worse, is still carping away about how Lucifer is the wrong fellow for you when you're celebrating your fiftieth wedding anniversary.

The Application: In the rare instance where *you* have profound doubts and have had them all along, perhaps this trigger will actually cause you to reevaluate your choice. In this unlikely event you may confirm the allegation, and break off the engagement. But in a more typical scenario where you feel certain about your choice, you simply have to deny that what is being suggested is true. It helps if you do this with maturity and style. For instance, "Yes, I do understand you don't think that Lucifer is the best choice for me, but why don't we just agree to disagree? More coffee?"

The Trigger: Runaway Planning Trains

Denise told her sisters she had set a date, and within twenty-four hours had follow-up e-mails from them saying they'd decided to band together to foot the bill for the flowers and decorations, and that they were thrilled to coordinate the lot. "It was awful, because even though I knew they meant well, my sisters' tastes are pretty much the opposite of mine. All I could picture was some incredible froufrou over-the-top scene, like something out of one of those hysterical bridal magazines. I didn't know what to say to them, and it made me immediately feel the wedding was out of my control."

Sometimes before you can say "reception hall," some family member or close friend starts telling you what your wedding is going to be like, from the engraving on the invitations to the pashmina shawl they see you encased in. (You feel encased, all right.)

The Treatment: Apply Brakes Immediately

The Goal: To ensure that a celebration that is first and foremost central to you and your fiancé doesn't become a celebration of someone else's tastes, needs, and neurosis. (A celebration that years from now you will secretly refer to as The Ordeal, instead of The Wedding.)

The Application: Even if you and your beloved haven't given a second's thought to whether you're having a wedding in the spring or a wedding in the next decade, you are fully within your rights to say, "Whoa, Nelly," and mean it. It may require behaving like a stubborn mule yourself and refusing to talk about anything to do with the wedding without sufficient time to consult with your betrothed. Think of it like this—it's akin to that scene in cop shows when they tell a person "You have the right to remain silent, blah blah blah," as they're making the arrest. You certainly have the right to at the very least . . . stall.

The Trigger: You Have Doubts

Shelley was engaged for almost a year before breaking it off. She still feels bad she didn't end things sooner, but there were extenuating circumstances. "We had been through an awful lot together. He helped me through my mom's death, and I helped him through a long period of unemployment. We'd seen each other for several years, and he was such a genuinely good guy. And totally in love with me."

All that, but not the necessary "and more."

"At some point about a month before the wedding I was talking with a friend at work about getting married. She said that one of the best things for her about being married was that it was like falling in love even more deeply with her husband as the years went by. It brought me up short. I loved Sam, but never felt I was 'in love' with him. I thought the other things we had would be enough. In fact I'd spent months telling myself they would be enough. But with the wedding date getting so close it was suddenly a lot more real, and I finally knew that feeling gratitude and respect and fondness weren't enough for me, not without a more profound feeling. Breaking it off was a terrible thing to have to do, but I don't regret it."

Ideally doubts should be dealt with before any date-setting, bridesmaid-assigning, or champagne-cork-popping activities take place. The doubts may take the form of insomnia, crying jags, not returning your fiancé's calls, or recalling in vivid detail everything you really don't like about the guy. Or, everything you do like about the guy, but acknowledging it's still not enough to make you honestly say, "Of course I want to spend the rest of my life with him."

The Treatment: Soul-Searching

The Goal: To not end up married to the wrong person (or marrying for the wrong reasons), thus becoming part of the dread "50 percent of marriages" statistic.

The Application: Only you (perhaps in consultation with the people who know and love you best) can take this on. It requires extraordinary strength and honesty. This may be a time to invoke that old chestnut, "Marry in haste, repent at leisure." And as horrible as it may be to contemplate, ending an engagement is probably not as gruesome as the jilting-at-the-altar, or mere-days-before-the-altar scenarios. On the other hand, there's also the obvious—doubt is part of the human condition. Questioning a decision doesn't necessarily mean that the decision was wrong, all wrong. Only you can say where on the doubt-o-meter your concerns register, and act accordingly.

(Not) the Last Word

If this final scenario seems a little dire, well, that's because it is. Chances are a marriage that springs from a solid foundation has a better possibility of succeeding than one entered into lightly, or with a great deal of uncertainty. But relationships, as is true of most things in life, are a process. They forever lack the definitive "now it's absolutely perfect" status. So fear not. If you have undertaken to marry someone that you feel, say, roughly 80 percent of the time completely wonderful about, you're on the right track. Now all you have to do is try and avoid . . . Going Bridal.

3

But I Love My Family, Really, I Do

A Tale of One Family, as Told by the Bride

Until about four months ago—oddly enough, about the time I got engaged—I would have described my family as basically a happy one. True, they all can make me mental if they put their minds to it, but as we've gotten older, serious dysfunction only happens on occasion. What I didn't bargain for was that my wedding (or "The Day I Never Thought Would Come," as *chère* Maman called it yesterday— zing!) would be the mother, so to speak, of all occasions. It's like the minute I said yes some cork popped out of the bottle and every twisty little family quirk rose to the surface.

Case in point: My mother calls today at work, something she never did pre-engagement. Her opener is your basic, "Hi hon', how are you?" Sweet relief. But then she immediately slips her tiny dagger into the heart of the matter. Would I (no "please," I notice) use her mah-jongg buddy's daughter's catering business for the wedding. And could I look at their website while we chat to get an idea of their hors d'oeuvres "spectrum." She's so insistent (and I'm so guilty about dodging her phone calls lately) that I give in without even taking a potshot at "spectrum." Next thing you know I'm surfing

Ecstatic Edibles' home page and she's trying to engage me in serious debate about the merits of Asparagus Spears Wrapped in Parmesan Frico Chips with Lemon Bourbon Chutney, versus the Skewered Buffalo Chicken Tenders with Tandoori Celery. Do I ask what in hell frico chips are? I do not.

Naturally, just as I am enlarging a photo of the comely Duck Pastrami on Sun Dried Tomato–Infused Five Grain Water Wafers, "The Boss" slithers up behind me. Cringe. She hisses, "When you're through with your more urgent business, do come and see me."

Meantime Maman has adroitly segued to the table centerpieces, despite knowing we're using pebbles from my Long-Suffering Fiancé's family cottage. (My friend Edie started calling him "LSF" recently, which made him laugh. At first.) I sense she's trying to override the pebbles; she keeps pushing for floating pink camellias. I remind her that LSF has already hand-picked the lot (currently they're occupying all of our available kitchen counter space, I might add), but to no avail. Formerly rational Mother has become Mother-gone-crackers.

"You know how much I hate to bring this up," she says, sounding like Katharine Hepburn about to dress down the help. "But after all, your father and I are paying for part of this. We should have some tiny little say in the matter, wouldn't you agree? And frankly, the idea of rocks on the tables doesn't exactly seem the height of elegance, does it?"

I babble something about The Boss needing to see me, hang up, collapse on the keyboard. Not a lie—no doubt The Boss has her stopwatch running. But I know if I don't unload the latest I'll go stark raving. Speed dial!

Twenty-five minutes later I've recounted my mother-daughter tête-à-tête to friends and fellow brides Edie and Priya (Angela was selfishly out of her office and didn't even pick up on her cell) when the woman across the hall sticks her head around the door. She has her living-vicariously face on, and whispers that The Boss is on the warpath. (I confess I've never actually liked this chick much but I took her into my confidence one day when wedding planning made me desperate to vent around the water cooler. Now she seems to feel this makes us best buds, and it's true I feel a certain obligation to walk her chapter and verse through the latest developments.) But just as I begin to update her the phone rings. I'm thinking, "Ecstatic Edibles with an estimate, please God no," but thankfully it's just my sister. Except now it seems even she's crossed over to the dark side, dispensing with the normal preliminary of hello. Instead she launches this baby at me: "I think you should apologize to Our Mother, she's very upset about the way you're avoiding dealing with the wedding. Oh, and this *is* a good time to talk about my dress, isn't it?"

Happy Families?

You may be one of the lucky ones who thinks your family is the coolest. You believe the person who said "You can choose your friends, but not your relatives" was a sad sack. You know that *your* family, who are thrilled at the news you're getting married, will be nothing but supportive. Or conversely you know in a New York minute that as soon as your family gets wind of your plans they'll want to interfere every step of the way. Truth is, sister, wherever your family falls in the laid-back to completely controlling spectrum, they'll want to be involved to some degree in your wedding. And you pretty much have to marshal their involvement, like it or not.

Unless your family is (and if so we're sorry to hear it) estranged, you probably want to share your happiness with them. But the process of planning a wedding may be the biggest test ever of your ability to cope compassionately with the many moods of Mom et al. Not to mention providing a crash course in learning when to pick your battles. There's a good chance that family more than anyone else will nudge you (or shove you as the case may be) in the direction of Going Bridal. But fear not; with a little thought, a lot of tongue biting, and some gracious maturity you may not even know you possess, you can minimize the Family-Induced Going Bridal moments.

The Familiar Familial

No matter how savvy a bride you are, it's possible that the full extent of Family-Induced Going Bridal will not immediately be transparent. No, the crystal-clear picture may take a little time to emerge from the clouds of newly-engaged oblivion. But take it as almost a given that if you are involving your family in the wedding—that is to say, not running off to Vegas—likely you'll have their emotions as well as your own to contend with. (In fact, even if you *are* running off to Vegas, since eventually you'll come home.)

Unless you've been living in cloud cuckoo land, you are at the very least forearmed with years of intimate knowledge of family cause and effect. Of the little and not-so-little ways your clan has of pushing your emotions around like pawns in an invisible chess match. However, you certainly can be forgiven for not understanding in advance just how abnormally cluttered the emotional chessboard may become in the days and months leading up to your wedding.

It would be foolish to think that just because you are getting married—a happy event—you will suddenly become impervious to the slings and arrows of outrageous family members. But at the very least, you can be the one who takes the high road. The one, as you may smugly tell your friends, who is being "the bigger person." Your ability to show restraint is partly because you are, after all, presumably still in the flush of just-set or finally-set-the-date freshly minted happiness. There's nothing like being all squishy romantic to make a girl benevolent. Still, that benevolence will be mightily tested over the wedding planning days, weeks, months, or (for a few unfortunates) years.

The Mom Goes Mad, the Bride Goes Bridal

The biggest test of all may come from the matriarch of the family, a.k.a. Maman, Mumsy, la Mom—whatever you affectionately called her pre–wedding planning. It may pay to remember, if you are starting to feel less endeared as the wedding plans approach warp speed, that your mother, a.k.a. she-who-is-being-annoying, is also she-who-brought-you-into-this-world. (Thus enabling you to marry at all.) Nonetheless, given the prolific nature of mom-induced incidents of Going Bridal, a significant portion of this chapter is devoted to the maternal source of the condition.

For mothers who do not give a toss whether their daughter gets married in a church, an airplane hangar, or not at all, the stereotype of the controlling, obsessive, wedding-crazed mother is unfortunate at best, disrespectful at worst. But sad to say, moms of the world, that stereotype is there for a reason. The litany of mother-related wedding horror stories is vast, added onto daily via Internet wedding site message boards. For example:

"My mother says if I marry Brad she'll never speak to me again. She met his parents and took an instant dislike to them. She coped with that by getting really drunk, on their tab no less. Completely embarrassing and upsetting. Even worse, she left before we'd finished dinner, crying."

"My mom and I have never been close, but ever since I told her I was getting married it's like she wants to make up for lost time. I'm a grown woman, I've got a kid of my own! I don't need her to help me decide on the guest list. And she keeps pestering me to register. We've already lived together for five years, I really can't see asking my friends to give us a toaster at this point."

You could spend a lost weekend, should you wish to, wallowing in the troubles other brides have with their moms . . . but you don't want to do that. You just don't want to let yours make you . . . Go Bridal.

It's My Wedding, No, It's *My* Wedding

If you know your mother is what might be called, conservatively speaking, "the controlling type," you know you are in for the match to beat all matches. You may ask yourself, indeed you may ask perfect strangers, why is it so important to your mother to exert this effort to control the wedding when it is so clearly your baby, so to speak. (Could one of the answers be contained in the question? After all, who is *her* baby?)

No doubt there are numerous reasons for weddings being such catalysts for control freaks. One reason isn't so bad. Unless you're dealing with Mommie Dearest, part of this frenzy comes out of love. She loves you, she's excited for you; she wants to share this really quite major life turning point with you. It's just that her love may become distorted through the other issues that weddings call up like dross from the bottom of a murky sea. Or, to use the vernacular, baggage. Some of your mother's baggage will be supremely knowable, the stuff you bitch about to your siblings. But there may also be a whole set of mismatched suitcases back there you knew nothing about.

One of the keys to avoiding letting your mother's issues make you Go Bridal is compassion. You need to expend at least a little energy understanding what drives her and make some allowance for her needs. If that sounds too lofty, put it this way—The Mom going wiggy may get to you, but compassion will prevent her behavior from making you . . . Go Bridal.

Love is, as we are constantly told but often neglect to acknowledge, complicated. It's not terribly rational and it behaves in mysterious ways. The need to control may well be seen by your mother as making a valid contribution to your wedding (weird concept, we know) and as a way of demonstrating that love. She may also be feeling some of her own sadness that this rite of passage means you really, truly aren't her little girl any more. (Even if you are well into your third decade and haven't lived with her since you were a Girl Scout.) Or perhaps she's trying to create for you the wedding she always wanted but never had—and this she sees as a genuine gift.

Now getting back to that compassion thing. You're feeling it, good. But at the same time you don't want to be the proverbial doormat. Mud does not go well on white, or even off-off-off-white. So when, for instance, your mother calls you for the tenth time to tell you to forget about the previous twenty caterers she's suggested now that she's found the perfect one, you may find yourself exhibiting definite, and not particularly welcome symptoms of Mom-Induced Going Bridal.

Diagnosing Mom-Induced Going Bridal: The Symptoms, the Triggers, the Treatments, the Goals

Symptoms of Mom-Induced Going Bridal
- Reverting to old habits of the nail-biting, hair-playing, and cuticle-picking variety during mother-daughter chitchats.
- Hot flashes. Similar to the ones described on medical sites you've surfed when you were trying to determine whether you are perimenopausal at thirty-four, or just get mad a lot.
- Seeing her number pop up on call display several times in a row but not answering. (Forget it, she'll know you're screening. Besides, how many messages from your mother saying "I know you must be there, call me as soon as possible" do you really want to wade through?)

- You start complaining, regularly, to your other loved ones about how your mother seems to have gone bonkers over the wedding, and it's making you feel like you're going bonkers too. (No, scratch "complaining, regularly" and substitute "complaining, obsessively.")
- You begin addressing people you formerly thought of as work colleagues as if they were close friends. This enables you to start complaining (obsessively) during your workday about your mother.
- She calls you at work, again, and you find yourself shrieking, "I can't talk about this right now," causing all your new best friends at the office to come to the door and say, knowingly, "Mumsy again?" And then you burst into tears.
- Your Long-Suffering Fiancé, a.k.a. LSF, makes you a beautiful romantic dinner and you can't finish your chilled quail appetizer because your mother told you she thinks chilled quail appetizers would be the perfect starter on The Day. In fact you can't finish any of your dinner, only the wine. And then you burst into tears.
- LSF has you locked in your favorite passionate embrace and at the crucial moment you pull away, exclaiming, "Oh my God, I promised my mother I would meet her at the caterer's this afternoon and I'm going to be late." And then you burst into tears.

The Trigger: Dialing for Daughters

Mary had always been one for brief regular phone chats with her mother at work. Nothing detailed or significant, just a "Hi, love you," and maybe a quick kvetch about mutual pet peeves. Thus it took her aback that once she began to plan her wedding her mother considerably amped up the frequency of those phone calls. "It was as if she wanted to live through the wedding planning with me. It got so out of hand that I ended up losing it, accusing her of living vicariously through me. She cried. I cried. And the ridiculous thing was I didn't even care about all that wedding stuff nearly as much as she did. But still I cared enough that I wanted to be the one making the decisions."

The constant phone calls are one of the most common triggers for Mom-Induced Going Bridal. Ideally they must be stopped at their onset. It is wise to recognize that the best defense against Going Bridal is, after all, preventive medicine. Any time one can see in advance what the triggers may be, one can try and reduce their efficacy.

The Treatment: The Preemptive Strike

The Goal: To strike at least a tolerable if not happy medium, and thus avoid both alienating your mother, and . . . Going Bridal.

The Application: Screening your calls really is not the best option, although it may be used at discreet intervals. Better still to have a conversation—yes, an actual conversation—about limiting her phone calls. (Or, given you're being "the bigger person" about it all, "our phone calls.") As soon as the calls begin in earnest, talk to her about reality. As in *your* reality. The one where your life is twice as busy as ever, what with the wedding. You may want to gently remind her that while it's true you are having a wedding, it is equally true you still have to work for a living. It's probably a good idea to emphasize that you do want to talk to her about wedding-related issues, it's just that you need time in between such conversations to give her "very valuable input" due consideration. You might suggest that ultimately this will be even more productive than, fun as it is, chin-wagging about the wedding every day. Perhaps you can set up a schedule—for instance, every Sunday evening you talk wedding. Perhaps not. But the first time she calls at a bad time you should politely but firmly let her know that it isn't cool, adding that you will call back at some other, specified time. And do so.

Alternate Treatment: Nipping It in the Bud

The Application: When Dialing for Daughters has been allowed to move into its preliminary stages, thus eliminating the opportunity for The Preemptive Strike, you may want to try this alternate treatment. The technical term for it is "Nipping It in the Bud." For example:

- *Please don't call me at work.* "Dearest Maman, there is a policy about taking too many personal calls at work. If I continue to take your calls I may be fired." True, this may fall perilously close to the category of the little white lie, but then much of life has a tendency to do so with no lives lost as a result.
- *Please don't call me before work.* "You lived with me for eighteen years, you know how much I hate talking first thing in the day." Or conversely, "You lived with me for eighteen years, remember how I used to love gabbing in the morning and was always late for school? They don't just give detentions for being late to operate on patients." (Or "file my story," or "edit my film," or "write my report," whatever.)

The Trigger: Just Let Me Take Care of It

Zoe was not keen on getting married. She would have been quite happy to continue simply living with her beau. But following a change of career plans, marriage was more or less foisted upon her for immigration reasons. Eventually she decided if she was going to have a wedding, she might as well make it into a bit of a splash. In the end it was more of a deep plunge, and soon she was in over her head with complicated arrangements. Her mother stepped into the breach. Sort of. "My mother had taken a totally hands-off approach to the whole thing, knowing I didn't want it in the first place. But one day when I was in a bit of a panic she quietly offered to help. I was so grateful I ended up downloading some of the wedding stuff onto her. But when she came back with the results I was shocked to see how much she had misinterpreted everything I thought we'd agreed she would do."

Your mother may, with all the best intentions in the world (or perhaps with some complex and not particularly savory motives), want to pitch in and help with anything or everything. She may want to help you with the following. She may want to take over virtually all of the decisions regarding the following. Or she may just want to gab with you about the following without doing a blessed thing. Quite likely she will single out one or more of these top five Going Bridal incubators—The Caterer, The Venue(s), The Dress, The Photographer, and The Invite List—and say to you, "Just let me take care of it."

The Treatment: Delegating Wisely

The Goal: To share with your mother some of the action (should she wish to be involved), without allowing it to make you . . . Go Bridal.

The Application: Calmly decide what, if anything, you would like your mother to do. And how much of it you would like her to do. Then let her know clearly, succinctly, and with a song in your heart (or at least no visible sulkiness) that you really do appreciate her offer of help, and that these are the things you would like her to help you with. Choose carefully. If she is an obsessive foodie who can never make up her mind about what to serve at her dinner parties, and all you really care about is that hot food is served hot and cold food cold, her angst about the chilled quail versus the chilled oysters in half-shell mignonette and lemon will ensure the only thing chilled on your wedding day is the finger food. You will be Going Bridal before the carpaccio hits the fan. On the other hand, if she is an obsessive foodie who will go off and procure the most wonderful chow, staying within budget and never calling you up to discuss preferred methods of marinating *coda di rospo*, this may be the task for her.

Or perhaps your mom is a real "people person" while you are somewhat less so, thus your chosen profession of lighthouse keeper. Consequently the idea of dealing with what the wedding industry calls "the vendors" (the people you buy stuff from) may fill you with horror. If so, why not let your mother gather vendor information, sorting out some of the options? (Unless she's the sorting-sort who is like a lepidopterist, where classifying and mounting the options on bristol board is a lifetime's work.)

Or suppose your mother has fabulous fashion sense—and gets yours—why not go dress shopping together? But if she usually greets you by looking you up and down and saying, "Why are you wearing *that*?" with a dismissive sniff, she may not be your best choice as wedding gown consultant.

"Just Let Me Take Care of It" Antidotes

Why let someone whose help you'd rather graciously decline make you Go Bridal? Here are some antidotes you may want to have on hand.

- *The venue.* "It's already taken care of." A tried and (potentially) true excuse for just about anything your mother or anyone else wants to do that you would prefer to do yourself. Of course, it helps if you have an actual plan. Otherwise you may be left dancing. "I, um, thought we'd have the party after the ceremony in our yard, actually. That's true, the yard only holds ten. But I'm sure the other forty guests won't mind taking turns."
- *The dress.* It seems obvious that The Dress should be the absolute domain of The Bride. (After all, you do manage to successfully clothe yourself day in day out.) This doesn't stop many people from wanting a say. You could try and negate that "say" with the never-unfashionable little white lie. For example,

"Remember how I helped to choose Destiny's dress? Well, silly me, but I promised her if I ever decided to marry she would help me choose mine. Yes, I know she ended up wearing a wet suit, but we're not getting married at the aquarium like they did."

- *The invite list.* A frequently observed petri dish of Going Bridal germs. Everyone gets involved, from those who wish to be invited and aren't, to those who are invited and feel the power. You and your betrothed should hammer out your essentials list before mothers or distant cousins or anyone else gets involved. Then if your mother wants her mah-jongg buddy Esmeralda to come, you can rightly say, "The venue only holds ten, we already have eleven." But be prepared to negotiate—especially if someone else is footing some of the bill.

DIAGNOSING SISTER-INDUCED GOING BRIDAL: THE SYMPTOMS, THE TRIGGERS, THE TREATMENTS, THE GOALS

Of course your mother is not the only family member who may induce Going Bridal. It's quite possible Poor Old Dad is actually Maniacal Old Dad, or Unendurably Rude Old Dad, or any number of other variants. But empirical evidence has shown that fathers generally stay out of wedding planning more than mothers (which may well be a blessing). Sisters, on the other hand, are often another trigger to a Going Bridal breakout.

And as with any family member, whatever your lifelong history is to date, it may well reverberate yet again during the heightened emotional time of wedding preparation.

You're one lucky gal if you're close to your sister, there is no sweeter friendship. But many a sister relationship is more of the Cinderella-with-the-steps variety. If you assume getting married is going to make the relationship better, well, chances are that's like assuming that having a baby will save a disastrous marriage. However, given the bride is constantly reminding herself of how lucky she is to be in love and to be planning a celebration of that love (you are reminding yourself, aren't you?), it behooves her to try her best. Still, you'll know when your sister is starting to make you Go Bridal.

Symptoms of Sister-Induced Going Bridal

- She says, "I think you should _____" (fill in the blank) and you hold the phone receiver away from your ear.
- You start obsessing with your friends about all the wrongs their sisters ever inflicted on them when they were six years old, and one-upping their stories each time.
- She's the pretty one and when she says to you, unconvincingly, that the dress you've chosen "does wonders for your skin tone," you feel like smacking her with that stack of bridal magazines she gave you and you never read.
- You ask her to make the toast and for the next two weeks she e-mails you with variations on the following theme: "I'm sure you really would prefer one of your friends do the toast, wouldn't you?" Instead of going into emphatic denial, you think, "Yeah, she's right, and why the hell did I ask her anyway?"
- She tells you that your LSF isn't good enough for you, and you feel like a cartoon character about to explode and ricochet all over the bridal boutique she forced you into, where you are currently being fitted for a dress she picked that looks like something out of a bad 1980s made-for-TV movie.

The Trigger: You'll Get It Wrong

Nicole says that getting married put her own relationship with her sister to the ultimate test. "All my life my sister has known how to make me mental. More than my mom, actually. If I said black, she said white. I knew as soon as I said we were getting married she'd start trying to make me feel like I didn't know what I was doing, because that's what she always does."

Generally this trigger is the purview of older sisters, who really know how to line up their sights. But that's not always the case. Sometimes it's the domain of the favorite child, whether older or younger. (And hey, no one wants to admit it, but many parents have a fave.) The wedding may well be a stage upon which to perform that old squabbling-sibs drama one more time. Whether it's a case of rank or family role, if there has been a lifetime of "sister knows best," what better time for her to know it than when you are making the biggest public statement of your fully formed adult self to date? Consequently, she may tell you that you have done any of the following:

- You've chosen the wrong man.
- You've chosen the right man, at the wrong time. (As in, "But you were just making a name for yourself slinging burgers in Tonawanda, and now you're throwing it away so he can play jazz in Paris? Who cares that he's smart, compassionate, funny as hell, adores you, and has an international recording deal?")
- You've hurt your parents' feelings, again. (As in, "But you know they're devout Unitarians and you're getting married in an Anglican church. They'll never get over it (again).")
- You've chosen a bridesmaid dress that makes her look fat. Or, you've chosen your dress so that her dress will look frumpy beside it. Or, you haven't chosen a dress at all—you are so foolish as to believe your favorite pantsuit you were wearing when you met your future hub will be appropriate on your wedding day.
- You've forgotten _____. (Fill in the blank: her favorite brand of bubbly, the maid of honor gift, the rice that she and no one else wants to throw.)

The Treatment: Just Let It Go

The Goal: To avoid resorting to childhood tactics of trying to hit her in the gut as she puts one hand on your forehead so that you can't get within striking range. Or the adult equivalent . . . Going Bridal.

The Application: This is one of the most challenging interventions between you and Going Bridal. Self-discipline is essential in many potential Going Bridal situations, but often sisters require a high dosage. Just Let It Go calls for great determination, a.k.a. tongue biting. So she thinks you chose to have your wedding in the rumpus room of your former roommate's parents' house to spite your own parents. If you know she couldn't be more wrong, who cares if that's what she thinks? You won't change her thinking. The only thing you can do in that situation is recognize that it is her problem, and stay focused on all the good things in your life. Remember, you're the one planning to marry that man who loves you dearly, and you and he are going to have the kind of wedding you want.

Just Let It Go Training Ground

- *Yoga class.* Downward Dog versus potential bitch!
- *The boxing ring.* First rule of fight club is don't talk about your wedding.
- *The mantra.* For example, you could try the always popular "Will this matter in fifty years?" You might also consider the pithy "Just ignore her," repeated at five-minute intervals.
- *Recalling your own successful choices and decisions.* Perhaps planning to marry someone you truly love who truly loves you might enter into this pleasant reverie.
- *Reminding yourself who you are.* One professional ballplayer admitted telling himself as he walked to the batter's box amidst the jeers of the crowd, "I am a professional ballplayer. I am a professional ballplayer." (Of course, you can substitute your

own profession or accomplishment. "I do make fabulous macramé hangings. I do make fabulous macramé hangings" will work just as well.)

The Trigger: You Like Your Friends Better Than Me

Karen, much to her distress, experienced this trigger quite unexpectedly. "My sister was visibly shocked when I asked her to be my maid of honor. Then she quickly tried to hide her shock by being overly enthusiastic about the whole thing. That lasted about a minute. Next she got really moody and kept saying all these really self-deprecating things. Finally we had a big blowout when she started being really bitchy to my friends. Eventually it dawned on me that she felt they were more important to me than she was."

This trigger stems from the insecurities and competitions of childhood, the time when someone designated her as the pretty one and you as the smart one or vice versa. It should come as no surprise really (and yet so often it does) that as you plan your wedding, she may well recall how in high school when she wanted to go with you to that party, you got all embarrassed and didn't want her to tag along for fear she would impede your social progress. Or she may brood about the times she's gone home following your adult parties feeling like a loser, given she's an aspiring floral arranger and your crowd runs to entomologists. Perhaps she's long harbored a strong dislike of every best friend you've ever chosen. She finds it difficult that your current best is a woman who does sex demonstrations for women-only gatherings in community hall basements, since as a gynecologist this completely offends her sense of propriety. Whatever the case may be, if she feels in any way either inferior or superior to your friends, if she feels there is a history of being uncomfortable in your social milieu, it may well be the fuel to her fire that ignites you in turn and suddenly you're . . . Going Bridal. This trigger usually takes one of four forms:

1. She suggests you don't really want her to do something you've asked her to do. As in, "You really want your friend Destiny to make the chilled quail appetizer, you only asked me because you feel sorry for me."

2. She refuses to do something you've asked her to do. As in, "I can't organize your stagette because your friends are bound to think I'll choose the wrong male strip joint. What, you loathe and despise the idea of male strippers? See, that proves my point."

3. She does everything you've asked her as maid of honor to do, but moans incessantly about the details. As in, "OK. So I called your friend Destiny to talk over how we're preserving the wedding mementos but she says you already told her you want the invitations pressed with fresh flowers in beveled glass. I think plain glass is classier. But of course Destiny would know best, being your friend and Esmeralda the glass-cutter's daughter and all."

4. You didn't ask her to be your Best Gal and at some highly inconvenient moment she lets you know just how utterly, completely devastated and/or furious this makes her feel. The worst thing to come out of her mouth? Something along the lines of "I guess this proves who you really love best, doesn't it?" (Note: under no circumstance agree.)

The Treatment: Reassurance, Reassurance, Reassurance
The Goal: To not end up saying, "You know what, you're right. My friends know me better than you, and I only asked you to do these things because Mom told me to," or some variant on that theme. What you don't want is a loving gesture to end up backfiring, with you Going Bridal to such a degree that after the wedding you and your sister don't speak for a year. (And there's not a single picture of her on The Day where she doesn't look like she'd rather be buried wearing periwinkle blue than be at your wedding.)

The Application: Now here's the catch. You may have asked your sister to do whatever it is you asked her to do because even though you know you are not as close as might be ideal, you do love her. She's your sister and you want to share your wedding with her. Plus, even though you may have had a lifetime of sibling rivalry, you want to try to use the wedding as a bonding device. As pointed out earlier, this is very ambitious and not likely to have the fully formed success you may dream of. But it may actually improve your relationship to a degree. And it certainly will make her realize you do, despite any age-old tensions, love her.

Consequently, the best response to the You Like Your Friends Better Than Me trigger is to reassure her it isn't so. She may say, "Destiny is closer to you and she should be the one to choose the color of the plastic swan favors, not me." And you should say, "Sister, it ain't so. You've got as good an eye for plastic swan favor colors as anyone. That's why I asked you to check out the swans."

The Trigger: They Always Loved You Best

Alexis is the youngest of four and she will admit, when pressed, that from time to time in childhood she sensed that she was a bit of the apple in her parents' eye. She considered it a product of being the youngest, a fringe benefit that evaporated once she achieved the age of majority. Until she started planning her wedding. "My sisters were really pissed. They couldn't believe our parents were footing the entire bill for my wedding, which wasn't the case for their weddings. They refused to see that it was because of a change in circumstance (my parents had unexpectedly inherited some money), and basically told me they felt it was evidence that I was being favored, as always."

For siblings to whom self-confidence was innate, for siblings who launched themselves into the world with more or less equal vigor and astonishing bravado, this trigger will likely not enter into any Going Bridal scenarios. But in the event that there was ever a sister or brother of the bride who felt that *chère* Maman and Poor Old Dad used to really bring on the tea and sympathy for that well-coddled upstart, the wedding may just be one more way of rubbing their noses in their perceived Cinderella status.

The Treatment: The Healing Waters of the River of Denial

The Goal: If you'd prefer not to end up shrieking, "All right already, Mommy really did love me best. Why do you think she gave me, not you, her wedding dress?"

The Application: It is quite possible that if your sister says accusingly, "But you were the one who got the pony," you were not necessarily the favored child. You may simply have been the most persistent and your parents wanted to get you off their backs. Conversely it might be true that you were their little princess, their little angel, or whatever nauseating appellation Poor Old Dad landed you with. In which case you have two options: soft pedal, or hard cheese.

- *Soft pedal.* The river of Denial flows on, embrace its ancient teachings. This is one instance where encouraging your sibling to remain in a state of denial is potentially a good thing. Say to her, "You are mad. They never favored me. Every kid thinks their sib got the better deal. That pony? It meant nothing. Remember, you got the hamster first. Hammy meant as much to you as Spot did to me."
- *Hard cheese.* Acknowledge the truth. Point out that it's not your fault. You didn't force your parents to give you Spot and the saddle instead of Hammy and the wheel. Your sib may counter with something like this: "And now they're paying for your wedding even though you're forty-two and a divorcée." Simply agree. "Yes, they are. I don't get it, given I'm a suc-

cessful stockbroker and LSF has another bestseller on the charts, but Poor Old Dad insisted."

The soft-pedal option is of course a better path to not Going Bridal. It may involve handing out tissues, martinis, pamphlets for twelve-step programs, whatever form of help you can offer as your sibling finally breaks down in tears, mewling, "Mommy always loved you best." But if she continues to persist in playing her tiny violin for absolutely no reason, you need to refer back to the treatment Just Let It Go.

Diagnosing "Modern Family"–Induced Going Bridal: The Symptoms, the Triggers, the Treatments, the Goals

They're shaken, stirred, but not always blended. Indeed, twenty-first century modern families frequently exhibit remarkable and challenging diversity. Many of us will be familiar with tales of someone's Thanksgiving dinner where not only the matriarch's current husband was present, but so was her ex, their mutual kids, and the tots that came along with the ex's second wife. Or about the teens who revel in having four sets of grandparents (including the steps). And certainly there are families outside the traditional "picket fence and 2.5 diminutives" demographic who get along perfectly well in their new configurations, thank you very much.

You may also know of a bride (perhaps yourself) who is in the process of creating a new instant family, where there are preexisting moppets on the scene. And if so, no matter how charming said young folks may be, you will know there ain't no such thing as Brady Bunch reality.

Issues stemming from so-called blended families can get particularly complicated when it comes to weddings. Weddings exacerbate "modern family" challenges because they enforce socializing that may not be welcome. No matter how acrimonious a divorce, no matter how confusing the "who-loves-who" epic has become, they all want to be there to celebrate on The Day. (And if they don't, you don't want them there anyway.)

If you expect Poor Old Dad to be there with his current girl-friend plus his last wife, and of course Maman, not everyone in that configuration may shout huzzah at this news. This is because they all have their own sets of emotions and issues with their current and past loves, just as you probably do. (Do you really see yourself invit-ing most of *your* ex-boyfriends?) Nonetheless, if you got to be best friends with Esmeralda, Dad's second wife, but also want to support his "dating at eighty" crusade by inviting his new "friend," and of course there's Maman, that's the way it's going to be. But recall that little warning—they may not like it. And human nature being what it is, people always let you know when they do not like something, either passively through someone else, or aggressively in person, where they suddenly unload: "I'm really not going to be comfort-able with Esmeralda there too, not after how she cheated at mah-jongg and then ran off with your father."

Symptoms of Modern Family–Induced Going Bridal

- A cousin looks at your fiancé's adorable twin boys, pats you on the belly and says, "Better get a prenup," causing you to con-template the following response: "Better find something else to do on the wedding day."
- The ex-wife of your soon-to-be-husband announces that she thinks it's inappropriate for her darling daughter to be a brides-maid. You desperately want to tell the ex you think it was inap-propriate for your fiancé ever to have dated, let alone married her.

- The six parental figures in your life all want to help with the wedding, just as long as they don't have to be in the same room at the same time as one of their exes. You find yourself wanting to decree, "Suck it up," or some other *au courant* equivalent every time you hear from one of them.
- You look at those pictures beside your computer of you with your parents, of you with your mom and Destiny's father, of you with Poor Old Dad and his fourth wife, and find yourself slumped before the keyboard with your head in your arms, weeping.

The Trigger: How Could You Invite Her/Him/It?

Glenda says she still gets a queasy feeling recalling how complicated her "modern family" issues became. "I wanted everyone there. I get along with both my stepparents really well. I never dreamed my mother would say she feels 'too uncomfortable' to sit at the head table with my stepmother. In the end it all worked out, more or less. But the negotiations leading up to the wedding were hell."

This is a frequent trigger to Going Bridal, when a parental figure in your life is distressed that you have invited an ex's current spouse and/or new progeny. There are of course other variants—the stepkids who do not want to see their "new dad" marry their mother, the former stepparent who feels he or she is too far out of the picture to feel welcome, and so forth and so on. Of course the issue of who is invited is sometimes eclipsed by the brouhaha over the wording of the invitation itself, especially when there are divorced parents involved. Maman may be so gracious as to accept that Poor Old Dad is going to be across the table from her with Esmeralda, but it may push her over the edge if the invitation to her daughter's wedding comes via her ex-husband and his charming second wife. In some situations it is logical to ask why parents, stepparents, or former stepparents' names have to be on the invitation at all. (Hint: they don't.) All of these variations on the How Could You Invite Her/Him/It trigger are best initially treated with the following remedy.

The Treatment: The Gentle Reminder

The Goal: To have everyone you want at your wedding without feeling like it's the unhappy business merger of the century, one that made your stock go down, their shares diminish in worth, and all trading stop while you . . . Go Bridal.

The Application: This treatment probably needs to be applied to yourself as much as to the other parties involved. Your wedding is about celebrating love. Specific love. Not their past loves, not their current loves. It's about your love with your LSF. And tangentially, their love for you. In an ideal world, that would be end of story. But there's nothing ideal in the world really (other than late-night movies with LSF when neither of you has to plan a wedding), so you may have to up the amperage and move on to the next treatment.

Alternate Treatment: Reasonable Negotiation

There are four steps to this treatment.

1. Acknowledge the aggrieved parties' feelings. As in, "Yes, I do get that having to sit next to Mom's second husband whose latest novel has been number one on the *New York Times* bestseller list for three months might not feel so good right now. Especially since your short story got turned down by *Small Town Fiction Monthly* again."

2. Try to come up with some reasonable solution. As in, "OK, we'll have your table on one side of the bar, their table on the

other. But I can't do a damn thing about dividing up the dance floor."

3. Asking them for their ideas. As in, "You know, I'm at my wit's end here. I can't help it if I like my mother's second husband, and even if I didn't I would feel obliged to invite him. Do you have any suggestions? No, disinviting Mom is not an option."

4. Tell them, as politely as possible (and ideally without using this exact phrase or one just like it) that you're sorry they're discomfited, but they are going to have to suck it up.

The Out-Laws

In some fortunate families, the in-laws are as loved as if they were blood relatives. Having a brother-in-law may be as good as having your own brother. (Or better, if your brother is such that you look at him and ask yourself, "Did we really have the same parents?") Mother-in-law jokes are of course the fodder of a million third-rate stand-up comics, so much so that people refer to them as a genre all on their own.

But just as the stereotypes about mothers and daughters and weddings (the mere utterance of those three words makes some exhibit Going Bridal symptoms), exist for a reason, so do the stereotypes of the meddling mother-in-law. Still, there are numerous factors at work when it comes to in-laws—for instance, interfamily competition, the age-old "our ways are better than your ways" drama, played out at many a joint family event across the land. Sometimes it is covert, as in "We'll pay for the rehearsal dinner, it's the tradition that the groom's family pays. What, there isn't a rehearsal dinner? You mean to tell me there isn't a rehearsal? This is your daughter's idea, right?" Sometimes less so, as in, "Oh, is that the kind of white that brides in your family wear, the red kind?"

Symptoms of In-Law–Induced Going Bridal

- Your brother-in-law-to-be, whom you secretly suspect is not your number one fan, refuses to be in your bridal party and you find yourself thinking, "Hmm, he really doesn't need to be at the wedding at all, does he?"
- Your mother-in-law-to-be, who normally stands as a shining example of how not to be the butt of mother-in-law jokes, drops by unexpectedly at work saying she is taking you out to lunch to "discuss" who should be on your guest list. You are so freaked that you obediently pack up your things and go, forgetting all about that business merger you're supposedly executing at noon.
- Your sister-in-law-to-be has a hissy fit because you only had your best friends at your "stagette," no relatives. You tell her, "For pity's sake, it wasn't a stagette, it was a small, discreet soiree." But she keeps pushing till you end up saying, "*You* might want to go to something called a stagette, I would not. So *now* do you see why you weren't invited?"
- Your LSF tells you that he thinks his family should be more involved with the wedding planning, and your response is, "Fine, why don't you marry them then." And you burst into tears.

The Trigger: We Just Want the Best (for Our Son)

Mariel, a young lawyer, was used to contending with sly barbs from her father-in-law-to-be. But he outdid himself right before the wedding. "We were chitchatting over cocktails one night leading up to the wedding when Geoff's father said something to the effect of, 'We raised our son to be a good citizen, not a lawyer.' Har har. Even worse, at the rehearsal dinner his dad gave me a T-shirt that said, 'Let's kill all the lawyers,' and when I didn't give him the big laugh he turned to Geoff and said, 'You sure she's got a sense of humor?' "

Even in these post-postmodern times, where the sexual revolution is a quaint artifact and adult life commonly includes a quest for sexual and/or gender identity, there are many things under the sun that remain as time immemorial has decreed. One of them is that there are still brides aplenty, and that the bride is, in most cases, the center of attention when it comes to wedding-related sagas. You may say to your friends, underscoring the irony with a visual sketch of quotes around the words, "It's my 'Special Day,' after all," but in point of fact in many ways it probably is. You may well have attended weddings in which this was not the case, but empirical evidence shows they are the exception. And the rule is one that sometimes irks those related to the groom. After all, what is their darling boy— chopped liver? He's the one they love without condition; he's the one whose future happiness is most important to them. And one of the ways this may manifest itself is through in-laws wanting in. Your mother-in-law-to-be may decide this is the time to tell you she feels you should be spending more time with her other sons, who are not in the wedding party. If you spent more time with them, she may point out, they won't feel "as hurt." Your sister-in-law-to-be may be bold enough to ask you, pointedly, how much moolah was splashed out for that Vera Wang, and is it true her brother is going to be wearing the tux he bought secondhand for a Halloween costume? Much of this sort of behavior seems to stem from a (rarely conscious) sense of being not quite the first-class flyers that the bride and her family are, of being the "B" team in the wedding game.

The Treatment: "United We Stand"
The Goal: To feel that you and your fiancé are even more closely connected than ever. And to avoid having anyone in his family come

to him privately and say, "Are you sure you want to marry this chick?"

The Application: The key to dealing with the emotions of the in-laws and your reactions in regards to them is to be able to communicate effectively with your LSF. Thing is, it's his family. Your prior relationship with them, good or bad, will be reflected back to you in that wrong-end-of-the-telescope magnification way during the wedding planning epoch. But ultimately the issues that will surface, like dross from the bottom of a murky sea, will be, to put it in the vernacular, baggage. Consequently your best hope in terms of not letting his family baggage make you Go Bridal is to try and be on side with your man in your approach to dealing with their quirks, their needs, their craziness, their style of doing things. He should know their "issues." After all, he's dealt with them all his life. He should at least have an inkling of which battles to pick, which ones are lost causes. Unless he is the happy-go-lucky oblivious sort where he simply accepts the way his family behaves as being beyond reproach. (The technical term for this is "mama's boy.") Either way, it may be up to you to instigate mature and calm conversations with him about his family baggage, even if it requires gently pointing out some of the patterns he may himself not have noticed before. Of course you could also choose to recall this pithy little axiom: "If you don't have anything good to say, don't say anything at all."

The Trigger: The More, the Merrier

"The thing that's making me most crazy with my fiancé's family is their need to have everyone together and in each other's faces all of the time," says Kelly. "He comes from a large family and I'm an only child, not used to all-family-all-the-time. Take my bridal shower, for example. I was pretty sure my best friend and my mother had been working hard to plan a shower for me. Then apparently they told my mother-in-law the date, which would have been fine, except she called my fiancé's brother in another state to tell him when the shower was, and suggest it would be a great weekend for him to come to town with his fiancée. I have no idea why she did this because she knew that it was a surprise, that it wasn't a co-ed shower, and that her son out west has a huge mouth. Sure enough, one morning he called our apartment and asked to speak to me. As soon as I got on the phone he said, 'So when is your bridal shower?' I was shocked! I said, 'I have no idea, I think it's supposed to be a surprise shower, and if you know something I would appreciate you not telling me.' No sooner did the words leave my mouth when he said, 'Well, isn't the date June third?' Needless to say, I was upset. This is the only bridal shower I will have and now the surprise is ruined."

The More the Merrier is the bane of many a bride's existence. Especially coming from the future in-laws, whose family ways and patterns may seem like a baffling universe in which transactions are conducted in a language that can never be entirely mastered. Naturally this trigger can be powerful, freighted as it is with the pressure of coming from the husband-to-be's family. Who doesn't want to say, "Oh, I just love my betrothed's eight siblings and all of his dear aunties and uncles?" But in some cases this may simply not be true. In which case, it is essential to apply the following treatment.

The Treatment: Who Do You Love?

The Goal: So that at the end of the day your husband will thank you for your patience with family matters, as opposed to saying what matters most is family—and you ain't it.

The Application: You might take a leaf out of Kelly's store of bridal lore, when she says she constantly reminds herself not to blame her future hub for his family's idiosyncrasies and issues. "I just tell myself that he is the man I love and what happens with his family doesn't reflect on him and all of the joy he brings to my life. I find the less I criticize regarding his family the more he takes my side without us arguing about it. I'm learning to respect that no matter what, they will always be his family and that his love for them doesn't mean he loves me any less."

Earth to Bride: Sundry Footnotes

- Remember, not everyone will want to help with your wedding; nor should they be expected to do so. To some people, decorating a bar for your wedding reception is about as fun a prospect as shifting boxes of books up three flights of stairs.
- You will not have control over how much any family member or friend actually does in terms of preparing for your wedding, no matter how much they say they really, really want to help. Remember, you are not hiring your mother nor any other relative to act as a wedding coordinator. Those people get paid.
- Sadly, money does enter into it. It is not an absolute equation by any means, but in general, "She who spends the greenbacks not only pays the piper but calls the tunes." If someone else is paying, he or she would have to be a saint not to expect some say in how the money is spent. If, however, it's your hard-earned money footing the bill, you need not be swayed from your choice of veggie pizza for all to feeling obliged to spring for dinner for eighty at swank resto du jour.
- Remember, at some level your LSF will probably feel protective about his family, even if he carps about them incessantly after every family get-together. Exercise tact and sensitivity about the in-laws-to-be, or you'll exponentially increase your chances of . . . Going Bridal.

AND THEY ALL LIVED HAPPILY AND
UNHAPPILY EVER AFTER

After all is said and done, you must realize that Family-Induced Going Bridal is, to use a quaint expression, "as common as dirt." This is not necessarily a bad thing, given that what is common can also be understood. And with due respect to Tolstoy, every happy family actually is happy in its own way. It's just that sometimes family happiness can get a little wacky. Sometimes love announces itself in ways one would never expect. (And yes, sometimes there truly are unhappy families containing people who are just plain mean-spirited.) But whatever Family-Induced Going Bridal triggers you may encounter, take heart, you're not alone. Besides, you won't be planning a wedding for the rest of your life! There's another handy old saying that applies: "What cannot be cured must be endured." Of course sometimes what cannot be cured might have been prevented or modified in the first place. And that, my dears, is the moral of the story.

4

FRIENDS, FOREVER?

A TALE OF TWO FRIENDSHIPS, AS TOLD BY THE BRIDE

SOMEONE ASKED ME THE OTHER DAY if it's odd that so many of my friends are getting married at around the same time. Unfortunately they asked me in front of one of those friends (that would be Edie), and I was so stunned I didn't know what to say. Because the honest answer is, "Why yes, at times it is a trifle odd. Some might say more than odd, perhaps even diabolical." Truth is there are times I'd swear we're auditioning for roles in *The Stepford Brides*. Gone are the days we spent hours discussing who's reading what, who's traveling where, who's sleeping with whom, and the other crucial who, what, where, when, and whys. No, now the only possible use for that consonant is . . . Weddings. It's pretty much All Wedding All the Time.

Which isn't to say we never have any fun being simultaneously engaged, as it were, in the wedding planning marathon. (Thank God Priya decided to elope in the end, so at least it's only three of us in full planning whirl. Think on that for a minute though—from arranged-marriage-girl to she-who-elopes. Her mother has gone completely mad as might be expected over this, but that's another story.)

The good bits of our three-brides-in-one experience can actually be very good indeed. For instance, there was the fabulous day when the three of us—Angela, Edie, and I—decided to play hooky from work and spend the afternoon registering together. I should point out that registering is a concept I'd barely even registered (har har) before now, let alone planned to enact. But Angela eventually convinced me of the wisdom of it. Although not before uttering these fateful snippy words in response to my resistance: "Who are you thinking of—yourself, or your guests?" My less-than-genial reply to that was, "Why myself, strangely enough. If I'm not mistaken this actually is *my* wedding." That particular exchange left us both cooling our jets for several days, but then she wrote me a very nice e-mail explaining why registering really did make things simpler for the bride as well as the wedding attendees. By registering, she pointed out, I wouldn't be faced with the horror of having to suggest to people they either don't give us a gift at all, or use their imaginations and choose something themselves, apparently both on the inconsiderate side.

In truth, the gift thing is something else I never even thought of when we first got engaged—I'm not in it for the loot. (Although I will admit it has crossed my mind since how nice it would be to have some 400-thread-count Egyptian cotton sheets. But then again, who among my relatives would spring for luxury linens anyway?)

No, there was just something that rubbed me the wrong way about the registering concept. It looked an awful lot like telling people you not only insist they give you a present (this after probably getting themselves new glad rags, not to mention airfare for four in some cases), but now you're going to dictate how much they will spend on it. Still, I eventually saw Angela's point. As she put it, "Look, they're going to give you presents whatever you do, so why not make it easier? Besides, you can always just say you want five-dollar drink swizzle sticks or something, and no one ends up going overboard."

Turns out the nicest drink swizzle sticks actually cost a little more. I should know, I've got a dozen down in the registry as we speak. And yeah, the sheets too, what the hell, maybe people can band together and each pay for ten threads' worth or something.

Anyway, the best part of registering was the day we shared—we had a lovely "ladies who lunch" afternoon, arriving at Ultimate Department Store feeling rather fine, and then spent a crazy few hours running around with these stun-gun things to enter our choices into a computer. At the end of that hysteria it was time for another feeding, then home gently to bed, feeling all mutually bridal.

So the multiple bridal life among friends does have its moments. But those moments are only one face of what I've taken to calling Schizo-Bride. That's because sometimes it feels as if Edie, Angela, and I are three mutating manifestations of some single bridal entity. A sort of seven-dwarves scenario narrowed down to three. There's Giddy'n'Happy Bride, Dazed'n'Confused Bride, and Manic'n'Frantic Bride.

For example, and yes, it's an example wherein I am not shown in a terribly nice light, I must admit, there was Edie's shower. Angela and I organized, doing everything we could to make it just the way we figured she would want it. Which meant as traditional as possible, because former alternative chick Edie went into her "If you are going to do a thing you must do it right" phase immediately after getting engaged, suddenly recalling her early Emily Post training. Where it concerns wedding showers this apparently means wearing little bows on a plate and watching your full artillery of female friends and relatives scarf down crustless mystery paste sandwiches. Angela and I (assisted by Edie's mother, although her assistance ran to saying "Oh dear" and hand-wringing for the most part) were up at dawn making said sandwiches and other delicacies. We planned all manner of cunning little shower games devoid of any indiscreet innuendos (and believe you me, that was tough!); we decorated Angie's apartment with more frothy girly gewgaws than you can shake a bridal magazine at. Both Angela and I were in serious Giddy'n'Happy mode throughout the event—perhaps aided and abetted by a few too many of the pink drinks (I noticed Edie didn't go so traditional as to say only tea was to be served), but no harm done. So I thought.

At the end of the day when we were congratulating our exhausted little selves after the last shower guest left, Edie decided to offer this postmortem. "It was lovely, guys, thanks. But I really don't think you should have been drinking in front of my grandmother and cousins. Yes I know, they were a bit tipsy themselves, but you two were hosting, and it just wasn't appropriate."

"Edie," I snapped, going into bridal personality number three, the pushed-one-step-too-far incarnation, "You would not believe how much we busted our butts for this. Since when did you become Doris Day, anyway?" But that wasn't the worst of it. The worst was what came out of my mouth next.

"If you weren't so obsessed with doing everything 'the right way' for your perfect wedding, you wouldn't even notice how much we did or did not imbibe, because you'd be too damned grateful we organized this thing at all."

I'd like to say there were immediate apologies and tears and hugs and let's-make-up. But the only tears were Edie's, who fled the room, and the only hugs were Angela's, who went after her to give comfort. And the only making up was one-sided when in the light of the following day I made my first effort, only to be told (fair enough) she wasn't ready to talk about it. Thankfully two days later she was, and to this day we refer to it as the day we "went Bridal" on each other.

WOMEN ARE FROM VENUS, WOMEN ARE FROM VENUS

Female friendships are possibly more complicated than the supposed Mars-Venus divide between men and women. And if ever there is a time for them to become übercomplicated, the bridal phase is it. You may wonder why, if you are the sort of gal whose friends are fonts of patience, understanding, self-sacrifice, restraint, tact, and so on and so miraculously on. Lucky you, if so your friends will likely never be a catalyst to any Going Bridal moment. This will be especially helpful if other people (for example, your family or in-laws-to-be) are providing those opportunities instead, thus giving you free rein to vent to your suitably shocked and appalled friends about the evil "others" who are making you crazy.

But for many women their closest friendships, even in ordinary non–wedding-planning times (remember those days?), are not without traumas similar to those experienced in their relationships with The Mom or with A Boy. This is a truism that is rarely acknowledged. There's a tendency to assume that the dynamics of women's friendships are somehow on a lower, calmer, less complicated plane than the dynamics between a woman and her immediate family or her love interest. Hah. Those assumers haven't paid the closest attention. Even a scan of fictional representations will indicate otherwise. Take Scarlett O'Hara, for example. Gee, what a friend she could be. Poor wan little "Melly" never quite got it, thankfully. (Let's just not even discuss Ashley's grasp of the situation.)

Of course there are also plenty of fictional examples of female friendships that go the other way, beyond (*well* beyond, some might say) any reasonable limits. Think Thelma and Louise. But to start on a positive note, let us take a moment to consider a tale told by one real-life bride who had some of the sweetest moments ever of friendship during the run-up to her wedding.

Isn't She Lovely

Some brides approached by the *Going Bridal* pack of thirsty journalistic bloodhounds were, frankly, astonished at the notion that there could be any bitchy who-does-she-think-she-is, don't-wanna-go-there stuff between friends during wedding planning. And we say, "tiaras off to them." What's more, in the spirit of vicarious living it seems only appropriate to celebrate their really quite lovely stories about really quite lovely friends. Let's turn the microphone over to Cathy, whose story probably best sums up this caliber of charmed friendship.

"Wedding planning without my friends would be like going into battle without troops! Over the past months my maid of honor and bridesmaids have provided tactical advice ('Get the off-white one, it's better for your skin'), strategic tips ('If you talk to both moms together, there's more chance of everyone agreeing'), supply chain duties ('We'll bring your shoes to the reception for you'), propaganda ('Everything's going to be perfect, really!'), and emergency assistance ('Yes, it's OK to call me at midnight to ask if purple flowers are going to look terrible'). Better still, when I was feeling too emotional or stressed to play the role of general, my maid of honor took command. Thank goodness, 'cause sometimes the general needs a day off!"

A word about Cath's stellar maid of honor. She didn't apparently expect or assume she would be chosen for the role, which makes this whole story even sweeter. As Cathy tells it: "I love my friend dearly and have always told her so, but she was a bit insecure in her female friendships, including ours. When I chose her as my maid of honor my friend's reaction was a torrent of tears, giggling, and Sally Field–like outbursts ('You really like me!'). She's much more relaxed now when we're together—it's like our relationship has finally entered into the committed stage. I feel closer to her too, and she is the most loyal, dedicated, and supportive maid of honor a girl could ever hope to have. So it's worked out for both of us, and I think our friendship has grown stronger and deeper in a way that's going to last."

Damn, wipe that tear out of your eye!

Now if your friendships aren't quite as golden, or are golden at times but occasionally show signs of tarnishing (particularly during wedding planning), do not feel the lesser woman. A computer-generated statistical analysis (what other kind is there—not a polite question at this moment) has shown that for every absolutely smoothly running friendship en route to the wedding, there is also one that hits a few potholes along the bridal path. Much depends on the women involved, their personalities, communication skills, and what their history to date has been. Let's take a look at the flip side to the charmed Cathy's girls story, with some words from Kelly about her friend Nina.

"When I got engaged, I called my close friend Nina from college. She lives across the country—I only see her about once a year, but we talk all the time on the phone. I asked her to be in my wedding party and she happily accepted, and even said she wanted to fly up to go dress shopping together. I should mention Nina is four years older than me, single, lives alone, and fears she'll never find someone to marry. Knowing this, I never really talked about my relationship or went into details regarding wedding planning. One, because she never asked. And two, when I mentioned my fiancé or the wedding she would change the subject or suddenly have to get off the phone. But still, I didn't think anything of it. So as planned, she came up to look for bridesmaid dresses and even seemed to agree with the final choice."

So far, so good, no? Read on.

"A few months later I e-mailed all the bridesmaids to ask them for their measurements and the deposits for their dresses. I heard back from all except Nina, until finally I got a call from her telling me that she had thought about it and felt she couldn't afford to be in the wedding. I was really shocked—I asked her if there was anything

I could do to help. I offered to pay for the entire dress and pair her up with another friend so she could split hotel costs. She seemed annoyed that I was giving her options and offering help rather than letting her off the hook. Still, she finally accepted my offer and we hung up. The next day when I e-mailed to see how she was doing, it got even worse. In a nutshell, she said she was upset at the way I acted when she told me she couldn't be in the wedding and that all I cared about was myself and my wedding and I couldn't give a crap about her and her financial situation. The gist of it was she wasn't going to be in the wedding and wasn't going to come to the wedding either. I e-mailed her back and told her I was sorry she misinterpreted my offer to help her out, and I was sorry to hear that she felt that way about me and about our friendship after eight years. This happened over two months ago and I haven't heard from her since."

Ouch. Now that story will probably bring another tear to your eye, one of great sympathy for Kelly, and perhaps for Nina too, since evidently she's no happy camper. But, sadly, Kelly's story is all too revealing of how sometimes friendships between women are far more complicated than meets the eye, with far too much that goes unspoken. Or gets spoken about in the worst way, at the worst time. And if this sort of friendship-unraveling event occurs when you are in the midst of wedding planning, there's a good chance it may make you . . . Go Bridal.

DIAGNOSING GIRLFRIEND-INDUCED GOING BRIDAL: THE SYMPTOMS, THE TRIGGERS, THE TREATMENTS, THE GOALS

Symptoms of Girlfriend-Induced Going Bridal

- You call a friend to tell her you're getting married and when she says, "Am I a bridesmaid?" instead of "Congratulations!"

you feel the back of your neck go "ping!" and you wonder if the phone cord will reach the medicine cabinet. (Recently stocked with extra-strength wedding-stress-sized painkillers.)

- You tell a friend you're planning menu options including roasted lamb, roasted chicken, roasted trout, and an incredible roasted veggie pasta dish, and her only response is, "What, no roasted soy products? What about those of us who don't eat meat, fish, or vegetables?" You briefly imagine serving fifty-five meals at the wedding, instead of the fifty-six that represent your actual head count.

- You're dress shopping with a friend and you turn to ask her if she thinks this one is "It," only to discover she's too busy trying on yet another pair of pants to give you the thorough response you need. And you tell her (only mildly shocked at your own petty self) that those pants make her butt look huge.

- You've been extra careful with the feelings of an unhappy single friend of yours, making sure not to "talk wedding" on your get-togethers. Then in the midst of performing your regular duties as sponge for all her woes, a passing mention of your fiancé causes her to break down in tears and moan about how unfair it is that she has nobody and you've got the gall to get married. Instead of doing the usual "I'm sorry about my happiness and I just know the right man is out there for you" routine, you find yourself saying, "Did you ever consider that men don't typically gravitate toward women who are weepy and desperate?"

- You confide in a friend that you aren't sure if Mutual Friend X will make it onto the list of invitees and she says, "The Right Thing to Do is to put her on the list, you were invited to her thirtieth birthday party, after all." You seriously consider making up a list of all the parties you've ever been invited to and telling your friend to track down every last host to make sure they can come to the wedding. Including those you went to kindergarten with, back in the old country.

- You tell a friend you're going gown shopping with your mutual friend, The Fashion Designer with Fabulous Taste, and later that day she sends you an e-mail saying how insulted she was not to be asked first. It's on the tip of your tongue to tell her maybe she should realize that the Boy George look has been out since 1983 if she is to be thought of as a budding stylist and dress consultant.

- You run into a friend on the street you haven't spoken to in years, and when you tell her you're getting married she says, "Oh that's fabulous, we'll definitely all be there," gesturing to her new boyfriend, his infant daughter, and his five-year-old twin boys. You wonder if you've suddenly become "the fainting kind," or it's just that the ground is that much closer than usual to your nose.

The Trigger: She's My Best Friend, No She's *My* Best Friend

Marie hung out with the same three women ever since high school, sometimes feeling closer to one than another, but always considering all three good friends. During the months preceding her wedding she found two of these friends were subtly and not-so-subtly pushing her to rank the degree of "good" in that good friend equation, thus establishing who was the *best* friend. It was an impossible and extremely trying situation. "Thankfully one of my friends was always cool," says Marie. "If I said I wanted to do something with one of the others about the wedding she never batted an eyelash. But the other two got very competitive. If they heard they hadn't been included in choosing the place settings or whatever, it was like I'd publicly humiliated them. There was all this 'What does it say about our friendship that you didn't ask me what I thought about the wording of the invitation when you asked her' kind of thing. It was insane."

Who was it that said "life isn't fair"? Annoying little statement, isn't it? An equally annoying, but possibly just as true and very much related statement is that friendship isn't fair. Sure, most women who value their friendships try to treat them with respect, but it doesn't mean there is some magical potion out there waiting to be applied in such a way that no friend ever feels slighted, annoyed, or disappointed by another friend. And when in the Busy Bride phase of planning, sometimes the bride makes decisions regarding her friends on the fly, without as much calm, reasoned analysis as per usual. Sometimes it's as simple as the bride thinking, "Hey, Friend 'A' is working around the corner from me today, maybe she'd be into checking out the plastic swan favors at lunch." Or as impulsive as, "I really need someone to view the Possibly Perfect Dress just one more time. Let's see, Friend 'Z' hasn't had a chance to weigh in yet." In other words, it's not always a defining moment in friendship when Friend "B" doesn't get to ooh and ahh over those fabulous plastic swans, and it's not always a sign of lack of love if Friend "Z" didn't get to check out the frock before "A" to "Y." And yet some friends will feel otherwise. Perhaps they will even feel as though you, The Bride, don't care about them as much as you care about the rest of the flock. At its worst this trigger may take the form of some convoluted statement that essentially translates to, "But I thought you were *my* best friend," thus reducing everyone involved to that sad moment on the playground when someone actually did say that in front of the entire school, leaving at least one poor little girl standing all alone.

The Treatment: Stand by (Me)
The Goal: To not end up on the adult equivalent of the playground (your living room, or worse, a public outing) with her claiming, "This proves she's more important to you than I am," thus endangering your friendship and making you . . . Go Bridal.

The Application: This treatment may be difficult to apply, especially when what you really feel like saying is "Grow up!" However, unless you actually don't feel at all close to said friend and see this as an opportunity to dump her (now that's *not* fair) you may have to apply this treatment. Not to yourself, but to her. You need to get her to see it really comes down to "Are *we* friends?" not "Is Friend 'A' really more important than I am?" This treatment can be applied by confessing to her how overwhelmed you feel by wedding planning (true enough, right?), and as a result how much you need some extra understanding from her, even if you have (in her eyes at any rate) goofed up. It's about asking your friend to stick it out, to understand that things are a little crazy just now, and you need her patience. In short, you need her to "stand by." She may view this as the emotional equivalent of being put on hold, but then you can up the ante with the addition of the third little word, "me." As in, "please stand by me." What friend doesn't want to be told that you need to know her love for you stays strong during a trying time? You may have to explain that even if you didn't ask her to examine the recently adjusted neckline of your bridal gown, you still need to know that she is on your side. And perhaps that matters just as much if not more than debating the merits of V-shaped versus Queen Anne.

The Trigger: Why Wasn't I Picked?

Some people are highly pragmatic, even when it comes to weddings. This sort of gal may choose her bridesmaids based on a carefully calibrated rating system assessing her friends' tendencies to be punctual, helpful, and accommodating. (Translation: they'll show up on time on the day; they'll jump through the vendor's hoops for you; they'll wear whatever you tell them to wear.) Other women choose the members of their wedding day festivities based on old ties. ("We used to take baths together when we were five years old and even though I haven't spoken to her since junior high, she's first in line.")

Still others make wedding party decisions based on some combination of head and heart. Take Jen, for example:

"I decided I didn't want to have bridesmaids at all. We weren't having a traditional wedding, and I thought it would be a bit odd to have my closest female friends, who range from thirty to fifty-five, standing in a row in matching outfits. But I did want good friends (including guys, I should point out) to participate. So I gave them specific duties in the ceremony, which involved doing readings, lighting candles, playing music, and so on. Well, much to my surprise one of my friends from work got her knickers in a knot over not being given a role. I was really taken aback. I didn't see this as the equivalent of asking anyone to be a bridesmaid, which always seems like handing out the Oscar for best performance as a friend."

Jen's situation is only the tip of the Why Wasn't I Picked? iceberg. And that can be one cold and lonely place, both for the lass who feels slighted and the bride who feels she's being iced. Plus Jen zeroed right in on a classic situation that makes her scenario a mere whisper of a finger on this particular trigger. Yes, for many people being asked to be a bridesmaid is a kind of validation of friendship. For such women it pretty much is like being awarded Best Supporting Actor. (Albeit probably having to share the Oscar with a few others.) The sad thing about this notion is it isn't always true. Maybe you've asked your fiancé's sister (whom you barely know) to join your merry little band as a significant goodwill gesture toward your fiancé's family. Possibly you didn't ask your friend who lives in Timbuktu because you figure she's a trifle far from home to go dress shopping. Conceivably you thought you were doing your recently and brutally divorced friend a favor by not asking her to be in a potentially precarious emotional spotlight by assuming the bridesmaid role. But recall, if you will, the road to hell with its pavement of good intentions. Regardless of your logical and compassionate decision making, some friend may well feel it is a case of the Oscars, where the failed nominees are left in their seats gamely grimacing in an attempt not to look devastated as some other chick is handed the statue. The sorry fact remains that whether you make a decision about whom to include in your coterie based on old loyalties, recent realities, or cold hard practicalities, there's one thing that's almost guaranteed. Someone along the friend chain may well feel she should have been the one making the acceptance speech.

You may be thinking this trigger bears a certain similarity to the previous trigger, She's My Best Friend, No She's *My* Best Friend. True, but Why Wasn't I Picked? does have its own particular set of manifestations, and therefore requires its own specific treatments.

The Treatment: Maids, Limited

The Goal: So that you do not cause any more pain than is already inherent in a Why Wasn't I Picked? scenario, and so that your not-asked-to-be-a-bridesmaid friend does not keep calling you up to whimper into your sleepy ears at 7 A.M., causing you to . . . Go Bridal.

The Application: Some brides choose the slightly eccentric and likely expensive way around the Why Wasn't I Picked? trigger by having every durn lady they've ever called a friend or relation-to-be on parade the day of, resulting in a cavalcade of bridesmaids potentially outnumbering the assembled guests. And it may well be less stressful to add one or two damsels to your fold, rather than expend your valuable time getting steamed about what so-and-so is saying behind your bridal back, or worrying if so-and-so will forgive you, ever. However, you might not want to go that route for any number of practical reasons. For instance, venue size: tiny. Or budget: you're the one splashing out for the swell bridesmaid getups. Style of wedding: utterly casual. And so on. If any of your reasons for limiting or altogether negating the number of bridesmaids are of this logistical sort, this is when it's time to invoke Maids, Limited. As in, "There's only space for one, plus me and the guy." Or, "There's money enough for two outfits, mine and my sister's."

If, however, there are no such logistical considerations, you may have to move onto the Alternate Treatment, the Blunt Bride.

Alternate Treatment: The Blunt Bride

Applying Blunt Bride is not the equivalent of Boorish Bride. In other words, being blunt is not the same as being inconsiderate or thoughtless in such a way that your words are certain to hurt. But it does mean coming right to the point. You must only apply this treatment as a last resort because rest assured, it will not be a piece of cake, given it is not topped with marzipan. No, your words will be the antithesis of sugarcoated. If, for example, you did not ask ancient-friend-from-the-past to be among The Chosen Few, because you only want the friends you feel connected to in the twenty-first century to fulfill those roles, you may have to apply the Blunt maneuver thusly. "Ancient-friend-from-the-past, I respect what we had together. But in my mind (perhaps not in yours, but in mine) it is from a bygone era. You do matter to me, and I do want you to come to the wedding. But I must tell you I have decided that the friends who are most active in my life at the present time will be The Chosen Few. Here, have a tissue."

Take another example. Supposing, like soon-to-be-bride Felicia, you have not included a particular friend in your little brood because you simply do not feel that close to her, although you suspect she views your friendship differently. Felicia admits she didn't want Friend X to be part of her pack, because X was a bit of a guilt friend. "I became friends with her at a time when I was kind of lonely, and I probably got more involved with her than I should have. I knew we weren't exactly soul mates, but she was someone pleasant who was always willing to go out to movies or whatever. Only I was pretty sure she saw the friendship as running deeper.

When it came to not asking her to be a bridesmaid, I decided I'd better tell her before she heard it from someone else. So I told her the truth, that I didn't ask her because even though we're friends, to me it was not the closest friendship, and I only wanted a few bridesmaids. Anyway, she got pretty shaky and teary, and I felt terrible. Then she said maybe she shouldn't come to the wedding at all if I didn't feel we were close friends. I told her I totally wanted her to be at the wedding, but that I couldn't pretend to feel something I didn't. In the end she said she would come, although she wasn't looking thrilled about it. But ultimately I actually felt kind of relieved, because not only did I deal with the bridesmaid thing, it also means our friendship in the future, if there is a friendship, will be more honest."

Felicia's example is a sound one. Because if you handle a Why Wasn't I Picked? situation poorly you may end up swimming in a sea of excuses, tears, character assassinations, and so on, when you would far rather be taking a luxurious bridal bath. And face it, hoping she won't notice she wasn't asked is probably not so realistic. Still it's your call as to whether you tell her up front, or wait for her to come to you. Either way, your motto will have to be "Be Blunt or Go Bridal." If you're overly cautious (in other words, if you're a wimp) and don't give her the straight goods this will not necessarily improve matters one iota. (True, it has proven impossible to measure an iota. But still, why waste iotas when you could be saving them for future Going Bridal treatments?)

Of course now you are pondering the seemingly imponderable, as faced by Felicia—how do you tell a friend she isn't the closest of all, when she, for some misguided reason, feels otherwise? You have to reach way down and find the words that will be least hurtful, but most honest. One thing to employ is a simple lesson they teach suits enrolled in management courses throughout the land: that it doesn't hurt to start with something positive. For example: "Misguided Friend, you matter to me, truly you do. You're a wonderful person.

But as difficult as this is for me to say and for you to hear, I actually do feel closer to the three chicks who are going to be swaddled in seafoam green. It's not a value judgment about you, it's just how I feel. And hey, at least you don't have to fork over the big bucks for the seafoam green. Here, have a tissue."

The Trigger: I'm So Sick of Hearing About Your Wedding

Lynn experienced this trigger to Going Bridal in a particularly embarrassing way. "One day I saw a friend across a crowded restaurant and waved to her, but she didn't wave back. I was sure she'd seen me. But then some of my colleagues came in and when I looked again she was gone. A few days later I saw her at another friend's and mentioned the restaurant thing. She blushed, and said she'd seen me but she just wasn't in the mood to talk about weddings. I felt like saying to her that I didn't want to hear about her work problems ever again, which had occupied many of our conversations over the years. It was incredibly awkward, it really upset me, but we've never talked about it."

Few brides, however casual and laid-back they are, don't at some point enjoy talking about their wedding plans. Or about how they feel about their wedding. Or about how they feel about the way other people feel about their wedding. Or about how they feel about the way other people feeling about their wedding makes them feel . . . you get the picture. It doesn't matter one jot that a million others have been married before—this wedding is your baby, your fingerprint, your special snowflake, yada yada yada. Sometimes this is hard for others to cope with. And quite frankly, this is something the bride herself can and probably should control.

The Treatment: Self-Censorship

The Goal: So your friends won't think you've turned into a hideous bore, and so that you won't perceive their possibly understandable irritation as hostility, making you . . . Go Bridal.

The Application: Yes, you may well want and need to talk about your wedding. After all, it's probably one of the more major parties you'll throw this century. But you don't have to (really and truly, believe it or not) talk about it incessantly. It does not have to enter into every conversation. Even when prompted. When someone at the office says, "How's the wedding planning going?" it probably doesn't mean she wants to hear about the heart-embossed table skirting you're mulling over. Do *you* want to hear about the cute little butterfly decals on her kid's diaper? Likely not. There is such a thing as keeping your interior monologue interior—and choosing what to say, when to say it, and whom to say it to. Which is not to say every bride needs to apply this treatment. There are some brides who find they too quickly tire of jawing on and on about who said what to whom over the invite list. These brides sometimes even impose "Weddingless Wednesdays," where one day a week they decree there will be no wedding talk, no wedding planning, no phone calls relating to The Wedding! You might want to take a leaf out of their Wise Bride book.

You Know Your Friend May Be Right When . . .

- You tell her a long, involved story detailing your latest shopping expedition for your perfect wedding delicates, causing her to plead, "Can we please have a conversation that doesn't involve either weddings or lingerie?" (And you think, "She's nuts, what else is there to talk about?")

- You ask her to come with you to talk to your mother about the guest list because you're terrified you'll revert to childhood and give in to your mother's unreasonable demands. Your friend says, "You're a grown-up, I think you should do this yourself." (And you reenter her name as "Traitor" in your address book.)

- Two days before the wedding you tell her you are panicking about the new fuchsia highlights in your hair, about the special

lighting the photographer said she'd bring but will probably forget, about this strange light-headedness your fiancé claims to be feeling, about the wisdom of having a wedding by candle-light—in other words, *everything*—and she says, "Friend of mine, it will all work out. You are going to have a fabulous time."

- You tell her that despite your long-standing deep-seated mistrust of wedding traditions you think you'll wear a poofy white dress and carry a bouquet and be given away by your dad because it will make your family happy, and she sits you down and says if you do, she will seriously question your sanity.

- You tell her that although you've always dreamed of being married in a poofy white wedding dress and carrying a bouquet and being given away by your dad, your fiancé thinks eloping would be a heck of a lot easier so that's what you think you'll do, and she sits you down and says if you do, she will seriously question your sanity.

- You think that wedding planning is making you hysterical and when you voice this concern she agrees and suggests that maybe, just maybe, you are getting a little too caught up in the whole wedding thing and need to regain a little perspective. (Damn, it's annoying when she's right!)

The Trigger: It's Not Fair That You're Getting Married but I'm Still Single

"When I was single, most of my single girlfriends and I had a blast," says Lisa. "But this one friend used to put a damper on any outing with some serious whining about her situation, like Ally Sheedy in *Betsy's Wedding* or something. I mean we all would whine sometimes, but she took it further. If I had a date and she didn't, she'd let me know how much it depressed her. If I had some foolish one-night stand and she didn't, she let me know she was thinking, 'Hey, what has she got that I haven't got?' And when she did have the date or the stupid one-night stand, she didn't ever seem to think that hearing every gory detail would have any similar effect on me. (Which, for the most part, it thankfully didn't.) Anyway, once I started getting serious about Gavin it was like just mentioning his name made her go all frosty. So I tried, I really tried to downplay everything that was going on. But then we got engaged. I still remember how much I dreaded meeting her for dinner to tell her the news. I waited until after dessert—I figured we might as well at least enjoy the meal. And sure enough, she started to cry, and let me tell you, they weren't tears of joy."

Lisa's story makes you want to wring your hands saying, "Oh dear oh dear oh dear," like the white rabbit—except no one was late for anything, except perhaps Lisa by not telling her friend sooner that actually it's not cool to feel barred from talking about what's really going on in your life. Not if you call yourself good friends. Which isn't to say you want to rub your single-and-hating-it friend's nose in your state of I'm-so-happy-it's-sickening, but at the very least you have to be able to talk about your relationship. To call a spade a spade (or, in this case, a fiancé) without fearing hysteria or sulking or bitter reprisals. I mean, c'mon, whatever happened to "I'm so happy for you?"

Indeed, that question is essential to the following treatment.

The Treatment: Be Happy for Me, or at Least Act "As If"

The Goal: So that she pulls herself far enough out of the slough of self-pity that the term *codependency* doesn't start to hover above your friendship. And you don't end up spending more time working on your relationship with her than you do on the one with that guy you're marrying.

The Application: When It's Not Fair That You're Getting Married but I'm Still Single is pushing your Going Bridal buttons, you may need to gently remind Single-and-Hating-It that not only should the quality of mercy not be strained, neither should the quality of goodwill. Surely if she is your friend she can be a teeny weeny bit positive about your impending nuptials? Or if she really and truly cannot feel happy for you, she can at the very least act "as if," as they say in some therapist circles. In other words, put a good face on it and not spoil any prewedding chick nights with an outburst of drama queen self-pity. Applying this treatment must be done gently, given she's clearly a sensitive flower and you don't want to trample her into the ground. But you do need to let her know that as difficult as she may believe her own situation to be, this is a joyful event that you want her to participate in, not one more reason for her to feel like crap. (And if she can't wrap her mind around that, hmmm—what exactly is your friendship based on again?)

The Trigger: Well, You Can Always Get Divorced ... and Other Cynical Remarks

Cathy, she of the wonderful friends, did have a near-brush with this trigger to Going Bridal but managed to view it in a positive light, seeing it as a good friend being supportive in her own way. "A few of my single friends are cynical about love and marriage. In the words of one committed bachelorette, 'I believe people should try everything once—and you've never been married so what the hell, it will be an experience. You can always get a divorce if it doesn't work out.' Um . . . thanks!"

The cynical friend who does not believe in marriage, or at least in weddings, may be the friend who virtually disappears in the months leading up to The Day. Or she may stand by, as in "stand by you," even if she does not share the values you are currently embracing. Or she may decide to gently tease you about any adherence to wedding traditions, say for example by bringing a bottle of single malt Scotch as your shower present instead of the household items decreed as theme. In other, less playful cases she may constantly rag you about your decision, threatening to make you . . . Go Bridal.

The Treatment: The Invocation of "Apples and Oranges," "Fish and Fowl," "Oil and Water," and So On

The Goal: To not end up after the wedding only having friends who think exactly like you.

The Application: This treatment is particularly useful in any situation involving a potential clash of values. Ideally it could be circumnavigated by simply agreeing to disagree about your differing points of view. But it takes two to agree to disagree, and your amiga may not feel like engaging in such diplomacy. In which case you may be forced to adopt this treatment, which requires pointing out the obvious—you and she are not clones, and it's not helpful for her to carp on about your differences during this stressful time. Perhaps you will need to trot out all manner of clichés about apples and oranges, about what a boring place the world would be if we were all alike, and so forth and so on. For example, suppose she calls you when you're in the middle of finalizing seating arrangements and your patience is obviously fraying. So she takes this as an opportunity to say, "See, more proof of why you don't need this wedding BS." This is when you may have to apply this treatment. ("Look, this is the thing. You see it your way, I see it my way. That's why we like arguing politics. Let's stick to the Democrats and the Republicans instead of the Wed and the Unwed, shall we?") If she suggests that you are "buying into a capitalist sexist patriarchal plot to make women subordinate clauses in the sentence of life," you may have to apply this treatment. ("Am I telling *you* to get married? No, I am not.") If she continues to needle you by sending you examples from websites detailing absurdly over-the-top weddings with the duration of the marriage that followed (as in, short), you may need to stamp your tiny bridal feet and say, "Listen, oh-she-of-different-values, I love you, but put a lid on it, already!"

The Trigger: You Aren't Seriously Going to Do It *That* Way, Are You?

Friends are close rivals of family in their ability to get that goat that's inside you just waiting to be gotten. Take Lina's friend, for example. She got married one year before Lina did, and consequently felt she had the inside track. Only she seemed to think "inside" meant "only," a variation on "my way or the highway." "When she was getting married I totally supported her emotionally through all the wedding planning," says Lina. "She has a lot more money than I do so some of her choices were things I could never consider. But I only gave her feedback when she asked me, and I never told her what I thought she shouldn't spend her money on. Even though I was shocked at some of the excesses, I just bit my lip. Now that it's my wedding she seems to think she should have editorial control over my decisions. And she acts like she forgets I'm marrying a struggling actor, not a surgeon like she did. For example, when she found out my sister's boyfriend was doing invitations for us for free, she said, 'No, not really?' in this appalled way. The next day she e-mailed me the names and numbers of several people who do hand calligraphy and papermaking, for about the same amount as my entire wedding budget."

This trigger is sometimes rooted in the belief (held by your friend) that she really does know of some option you may not have considered that would be just perfect for you. An option for pretty much anything, from the kind of sand you plan to have in your centerpieces to the words that are going to come out of your wedding officiant's mouth. But even if you sense your friend is offering you her advice out of love (not some age-old covert rivalry about who is smartest, sexiest, best-at-life-est), it can be wearing. You may need to respond to this trigger in the following manner.

The Treatment: Yes, I Am Seriously Going to Do It *That* Way

The Goal: To have a huffy friend who gets over it, rather than an alienated friend you Go Bridal on to such a degree that the only option left for her to present is the one where she doesn't come to your wedding.

The Application: This treatment should be preceded by a little soft sell, as in a bit of chat about how much you appreciate her good intentions. (If you suspect they're not good, you may not want to get into that discussion in the precarious prewedding moments—save it for after the honeymoon.) But then you follow "making nice" by taking that deep breath you're becoming well versed in by now, and delivering the truth—that you have made your choice and are stickin' by it. You may want to give her the background to your decision, as in, "We're going with the French sand in the centerpieces because it reminds us of that trip we took to the Riviera." Or you may not, as in, "Look, I'm too stressed to get into why we want to use the French sand instead of the Peruvian as you suggested. And you know what would be really great right now? Not talking about the wedding."

You Know Your Friend May Be Wrong When . . .

- She tells you there is only one "right way" to do anything connected to your wedding. (This is your cue to say, "Goodness, you didn't mention you'd written 'The Rules' for brides!" Or perhaps, "Say, sister, if you want to tell me about my wedding offenses you'll have to take a number.")

- She starts dissing your father-in-law-to-be who is making your fiancé's life hell, your mother who is making your life hell, and your mutual friend who is making both of your lives hell. (Which may, if you have your wits about you, cause you to remind her that venting and dissing, while equals in terms of syllabic construct, are not one and the same.)

- You tell her that you want to keep things as simple as possible and she says, "Great, then I'll call caterers and florists and dressmakers and wedding planners on your behalf, and arrange it all for you."

- You tell her you think you will wear that comely frock you bought in Paris last April and she says, "I can't believe you aren't going out and getting a dress specifically for your wedding day. You'll definitely regret that."

- You've got all the reception details set, from your sister's home-made Ritz cracker canapés to your adorable single-candle centerpieces. Your friend tells you that even though you think you've got it under control, that's only because you don't know what else is available. You must check out www.Bewilderthe BrideforBigBucks.com, the wedding website her sister runs.

- She tells you she is so hurt at your choice of bridesmaids, a club to which she has not been offered membership, that not only will she not come to your wedding, she thinks you owe it to her to give a detailed explanation of why you chose each of those cows.

Friends Forever, Enemies Never

Hopefully your Friend–Induced Going Bridal moments will be few and far between. Or at the very least any such incidents will be more than amply balanced by a veritable cornucopia of positive memories of fun, silly, meaningful, or otherwise good times shared with friends pre–The Big Day. And with any luck (and/or determination) you'll even manage to reciprocate the love and support your friends give you during the wedding-planning whirl. Because when you stop and think about it, there's a big-picture reason to continue to be a good friend to your best gals during the throes and lows of being bewitched, bothered, and bridal. That which lies on the other side of your wedding—a.k.a. the rest of your life.

5

Planning Is a Pain in the Butt, But ...

A Tale of the Logistically Challenged, as Told by the Bride

Yesterday I confronted my inner Lazy Bride in a face-to-face I suppose I needed to have. It was a confrontation brought on by The Intervention, as I call the little plan cooked up by *chère* maman and enacted by friends Angela and Edie. Not only are A&E going to be my bridesmaids, they also seem to have become my mother's hand-maidens, running interference for her whenever she knows I'm too hot under the collar for her to handle.

It strikes me as utterly bizarre that my mother, who barely knows Angela and Edie (it's not like they're childhood friends she used to make PB&J for), now regularly phones them to "keep myself in the loop," as she puts it. The loop that lately has felt a tad noose-like, tightening even further during The Intervention.

There we were, the three of us supposedly going for sushi and a movie without (gasp!) any wedding talk, since we agreed we could all use a time-out. Only we never got to the flick. No, just as I'm looking at my watch trying to assess how badly I really want that salmon hand roll and would it arrive in time to make it to the 7:10

show, Angela delicately announces, "Um, there's something we'd like to talk about." Uh-oh. Whenever someone starts talking about "talking about something," that spells trouble.

"Oh yeah," I say casually, signaling the waiter. Might as well enjoy a wasabi rush along with the other increase in temperature I'm beginning to feel—I admit I don't always take criticism too well. But it turns out it isn't exactly criticism coming my way, more like they've been studying up on conflict resolution: "How to Avoid the Battle of the Bride," or "Beware the Bitchy Bride." Yes, I admit I've been a bit testy lately.

"Thing is," says Edie, doing the tag team approach, "Your mother is kind of concerned about some aspects of the wedding."

"And we promised to talk to you, because we're kind of concerned too," adds Angela.

I decide not to tell them that I think "Aspects of the Wedding" sounds like an Ingmar Bergman movie, the kind where someone goes quietly mad, likely dressed in white.

"Basically, she's worried you haven't sorted out all of the details, the logistics, the vendors . . . you know, everything. And she thinks you're running out of time," says Edie.

"And she says when she tries to talk to you about the seating arrangements you just roll your eyes," chimes Angela.

"Salmon roll, yum yum," I say, defiantly rolling my eyes at that very moment. A good diversion, or at least it would have been were it not for their somber faces staring intently at me. I consider telling the old joke about a guy who walks into a bar, sees a mournful horse, and says, "Why the long face?" But even I realize that absurd kid-jokes will not turn this back into no-wedding-talk sushi-and-movie night.

So then we get into it. They plead with me to explain why it is that after my initial push to get all the wedding details set I just kind of faded, with about half the arrangements in place, the rest left twisting in the wind. My mother, it seems, thinks this is merely me being difficult. (*Moi?* Cut me to the quick, Maman.) But my friends have decided to sabotage our movie outing because they are seriously worried that my lack of action indicates something of a higher order. Something that signals, to cite the phrase that haunts weddings the world over, "Getting Cold Feet."

"My dogs are as warm as warm can be," I assure them. "No, there's something else stopping me from making all the arrangements, something deeper inside of me that will not be denied." They lean forward, clearly breathless with anticipation. And then I tell them my shameful secret, something that wedding planning, with all its convoluted sets and subsets of details, has caused me to try to conceal. I come out of my bridal closet and admit that it's true . . . I am the original Lazy Bride. I don't want to have to make one more decision regarding who will take the damned coats at the reception, or who will be seated with whom. Let them actually remove their own coats, and place them upon hangers with their own fair hands! Let them ease their weary bodies into the nearest chair! Let the planning not be such a pain in the ass!

"Oh that," Angela says. "So it's just about you being lazy with stuff as usual?"

As usual! Humph! Well it seems they knew all about my secret after all, what with years of me inviting them over for dinner and then ordering in, rather than serving them lovingly prepared gourmet meals. But they are relieved, mightily relieved, that it is merely "the laziness" to blame, not any doubts about my commitment to my Long-Suffering Fiancé.

Not end of story though, since suddenly they seem to view me as a project that needs management, something along the lines of When Brides Go Bad, Good Friends Get Going. They force me to make what they reverently call a To-Do List, as though it has more significance than any other, ordinary list. And as soon as the page begins to fill with what remains to be To-Done, I feel a hot flash I'm positive isn't a wasabi rush. I think my heart is palpitating, although I'm not exactly sure what that means, but if it could be palpitating it would be. I can't face all these details, the organizing, the phone call-ing, the bartering and brokering—and this was supposed to be a simple, casual wedding!

I try and recall the teachings of visualization: imagine what you want, then slip into "the calm place" where you can achieve that need. Edie and Angela, good friends that they are, enable me to articulate my vision.

"What is it you'd like to see happen at this point?" says Edie.

"Um, eloping? No wedding?"

"That's out of the question, so what's your second option?" says Angela.

"Um, a wedding planner?"

Together we look at the other side of the To-Do, where I've scribbled down the math pertaining to our dwindling budget and how far into debt we are willing to go, which would never in a mil-lion years stretch for a wedding planner.

They look at the pathetic figures, as do I.

"Read it and weep," I say. And then, most unexpectedly, I do.

The Devil Is in the Details

When you and your fiancé have that first conversation about your wedding day, chances are you don't discuss the dimensions of the croque-en-bouche (unless you both happen to be French pastry chefs) or the backlit table this creation will sit upon, waiting to be cut with your grandmother's nineteenth-century pearl-handled cake knife. In all probability most of the wedding details are much like the personalities of your unborn children—who cares whether you'll have a good baby or a cranky one, you're just dreamily think-ing "baby." That's because the "just engaged" state tends to make couples feel like "love's young dream," as the Brits put it, too besot-ted to fuss over any of the petty real-life stuff, no matter your age or how many times you've been previously married.

Cast your mind back to those early days. Before the word *planning* became The Evil "P" Word. At that time there was nothing that could rain on your parade, given that the parade was far enough into the future that it and rain could not possibly be conceived of in the same sentence. Oh sure, you may have spent a few starry-eyed candle-lits talking wedding plans. But those conversations were probably punctuated by the self-confidence of knowing that you're too savvy to get in a twist over what amounts to nothing more than what you probably take on in the average workweek—the management of time, details, and "the little people." You may have even heard yourself casually saying to your beloved, "How complicated can it be?" After all, what's the big deal: you score a venue, wrangle someone to say a few words, buy some bubbly, and voilà! You can't see anything about the logistics, or the so-called vendors (that is, the people who sell you stuff like dresses, cakes, and wedding receptions) that could be so monumental.

On the other hand, if you've witnessed weddings where some of those "best-laid plans" devolved with great rapidity and remarkable lack of grace, you may be singing from a different hymnbook. You may feel a certain amount of anxiety about your ability to find within yourself the wherewithal to make those best- (or worst-) laid plans at all. Take, for example, a young bride-to-be named Emma, who finds the very idea of wedding planning so overwhelming that she's simply opting out. Oh yes, she's still engaged. But she refuses to plan—possibly becoming a case of Always the Near-Bride, Never the Bride.

"Therefore, I Have Decided Not to Bother with Any Planning Right Now"

Emma is startling in her clarity about her perpetual state of Near-Bride. When asked as to why she has not set the date, she firmly states the following:

"Size. My fiancé would like a large wedding with tons of people—whereas I would like a quiet, intimate wedding. I would be happy eloping, him not so much. I would be happy going to city hall and then having a dinner party with friends and family, him not so much. Therefore, I have decided not to bother with any planning right now."

So Emma, tell us how you *really* feel.

"Then there's location. We both have family all over the map. Some relatives are in Toronto, some in Montreal, some in Dallas, some in London. Therefore, I have decided not to bother with any planning right now."

Is that it? Apparently not.

"Then there's free brain space. We bought a house last year and after all the planning that was necessary for the house I don't wish to spend my free time planning anything aside from getting ourselves to and from work and eating. Therefore, I have decided not to bother with any planning right now."

Emma finishes this dramatic monologue by asking, plaintively, "I wonder if anyone else feels the way I do?"

In truth, gentle reader, Emma is not alone. It would seem that indeed there are many Near-Brides out there orbiting Planet Wedding, wondering if they will ever touch down. Afraid that the very entry into that planet's atmosphere of planning may make them . . . Go Bridal.

The (Lack of) Time and Space Continuum

For all that Going Bridal is frequently a matter of the domino effect of the varying temperaments of all the good people involved in your wedding, it can also be prompted by matters of Time and Space. Or lack thereof. The logistics-challenged among us already understand this. If you're nodding right now, that may be because you know, in your heart of hearts, that you're a procrastinator of the highest order. The whole notion of adhering to some countdown/timeline to what is meant to be a joyous celebration just seems contrary; something to be avoided (if not downright ignored) at all costs. The aggravating concerns over how many people can fit into the wedding venue you haven't yet found? Ditto.

On the other hand, perhaps it's not a question of mere procrastination. Could be you're the sort of person who sees all sides to a story, and tends to bog down in deepest bog when faced with having too much choice. Thus the issues pertaining to Time and Space so intrinsic to wedding planning may also seem not to be your friends. You may become stuck in the seemingly endless orbit of Near-Bride as a result, trying, trying, trying (unsuccessfully) to find a date, a place, a country to hold your wedding.

Then there is another breed, referred to as Take Charge personalities. (Or at their most extreme, Take Over personalities.) If you are of this ilk you may become so wound up by manipulating the Time and Space considerations that your swiftly decisive actions result in unhappy responses from all the aforementioned good people involved in your wedding, which pleases you not at all.

Whichever camp you fall into (or halfway house you occupy in between), dealing with "Wedding: Where, When, and Who" can prove irksome at best. Still, you do have a choice. Choice One: you acknowledge that the importance of any Time and Space issues connected to your wedding are best summed up by the notion "it's all relative"—crucial to your wedding, yes, but solvable, and certainly not crucial to the survival of the human race. Or Choice Two: you believe (albeit on some deeply subliminal level) that the significance of these matters does actually rank in close proximity to issues concerning survival of the human race. A belief guaranteed to make you a perfect specimen of . . . Going Bridal.

DIAGNOSING TIME AND SPACE–INDUCED GOING BRIDAL: THE SYMPTOMS, THE TRIGGERS, THE TREATMENTS, THE GOALS

Symptoms of Time and Space–Induced Going Bridal

- Your closest family members live in one country, his in another, the two of you in a third. After yet another session with a travel agent trying to reconcile these differences you decide the best place to get married is equidistant to all three points, which turns out to be Climax, Saskatchewan, population 230. (And climbing!)

- You want a spring wedding but spring is when your betrothed is taking his bar exam, so he suggests it's a poor time for the pair of you to wed. You indignantly insist he's making his career the priority, and when he looks at you with disbelief and says, "It is the bar exam, so I suppose I am, actually," you huff out saying, "Well maybe we just shouldn't get married at all." (Followed by a tearful, embarrassed apology in the wee hours.)

- Your fiancé's immediate family numbers thirty, and your dream venue holds forty. Instead of recognizing this for the impossibility that it is, you find yourself snarling, "No way are those aunts and uncles of his coming, no way."

- The RSVP cards are still only trickling in a week before the cutoff date, by which point your relationship with your mailman is such that he offers you his hankie along with your pile of wedding-related bills.

- You want to seat your oldest friends together at one table, but your mother says she thinks The Right Thing to Do is to mix up the friends and family so as to encourage mingling. This is on the heels of her previous ordinance stating The Right Thing to Do is to seat friends and family separately so as to encourage a natural comfort level. You find yourself shrieking,

"The Right Thing to Do is to let 'em all sit wherever the hell they want!"

The Trigger: Location, Location, Location

Fran and her betrothed are both actors, and right before their wedding they'll be working at a country theater. (Ironically in a play about a couple getting married—what are the chances of that!) Anyhoo, they decided to get married on a 165-acre horse farm close by, and she's planning a huge country *ceilidh* to celebrate their Scottish and Irish heritage. "Celtic music under the stars," she says, "what could be sweeter?" (Perhaps having your guests refrain from bickering about where they will be lodged?) Here's Frannie, in the midst.

"I try and find a cottage or a B&B for our guests, then my loving and far too generous mum worries that it's too expensive for people traveling from overseas, so she says, 'Oh, they can all just bunk up with us.' A surefire recipe for chaos. Or she pleads with me to find something cheaper. Or the parents think the latest guest accommodation is too far away from the action. Or some guest inevitably says, 'It would have been so much easier to do it here . . .' Here being wherever that person lives, never mind that my fiancé and I don't live there. Or I reserve something and some other guest pipes in with, 'Well remember Catherine doesn't like so and so . . .' All I want to do is make sure everyone has a bed, they can sleep next to whomever they want!"

The location of the ceremony itself, the reception, the pregame dinner, the postgame brunch—any or all of these things have been known to pose moments of stress for some women planning their weddings. (Understatement, defined.) Unless you've known since the dawn of time that a certain religious establishment and a particular reception spot would be the site of your wedding (and you get some kind of award if that describes you), the options are indeed endless. Let's see, should the wedding be at the Loyal Order of Buffalo Lodge, or the Academy of Science's Hybrid Swamp Lily Garden? What about Bimbo's Crab Shack'n'Wedding Palace or the Roll-the-Dice Function Center?

As with many of the logistical issues pertaining to the condition of Going Bridal, Location, Location, Location can be treated with a return to one of those remedies Great-Granny likely called horse sense, given those sensible creatures know that whatever else fails, you can always go home to the barn.

The Treatment: The Tried and True

The Goal: So that partway through your wedding ceremony you don't have that just-woke-up-and-haven't-a-clue-where-I-am feeling, causing you to internally wail, "Why are we getting married *here?*"

The Application: Although the allure of an exotic destination wedding thrills some, others find merely choosing between swank resto du jour and swank living room du Ma et Pa as the locale for their wedding already has them destination-challenged. It goes without saying that the almighty dollar may indeed figure into any choice of venue, consequently limiting your options. But what about your emotional options? Obviously if you have to consider matters such as wheelchair access, and your dream venue is a building that only boasts spiral staircases, you may have to reconsider your choice. But short of that scenario, this treatment is about reminding yourself of what really matters most to you, of the tried and true. The "true," as in true to your heart. Where will you and your LSF feel most at home? It's thinking like this that may remind you that while your horticulturalist mother is pushing for the botanical gardens with those gorgeous scented Mexican frangipani, you see yourself marrying in your grandmother's backyard where the strongest scent is the garden-variety mint she planted with you when you were a small child.

Mind you, it's possible you have no such dear-to-the-heart locale in mind. In which case you could adopt the attitude successfully honed by brides the world over. The "It's only a site for the wedding, not the marriage" attitude. Then your decision more likely comes down to matters of budget and practicality.

As for the multiple other variations to the Location, Location, Location trigger (such as Fran's dilemma as to where to house her guests), they are best treated by applying something that also comes under the category of equine sense—summed up by one word, writ large: *Patience*.

For the Location-Challenged

If the seemingly infinite wedding venue possibilities overwhelm, consider the anti–Going Bridal advice of Ken McEachern, owner of Fantasy Farm (in the Big Day biz since the 1940s).

- Avoid becoming a Burned-Out Bride by doing a little prep before venue shopping. Sort out the financing first, *then* approach venues with a clear grasp of your budget and number of guests. If you haplessly visit the venue with no real clue of these matters, and ask them to name a price, guess what? It'll be more than you can afford.

- Avoid becoming a Bride on the Edge by recalling the old gut-feeling test. If something were to go awry with the logistics or even if (unlikely as it is, of course) something should disturb your typically calm demeanor, do you sense the folks at this establishment would provide an understanding shoulder to lean on?

The Trigger: I Think You Should Invite So-and-So

Can we just say this once? Before we hear from Hannah, who has an all-too-typical invitation list horror story? Can we just say that you are an absolute rarity among brides if the list of invitees is *not* a trigger to Going Bridal? And if it's not, we're willing to exchange gold bullion for your secret? OK, whew, we said it. Now let's hear from Hannah. It's a long story, but a good one. (Well, as in "good-bad.")

"Dave's father seemed to view our reception as a way to meet social and family obligations. He has a rather distant relationship with most of his relatives, which maybe he feels a bit guilty about. He also spent years attending the weddings of his law partners and other colleagues without reciprocating. This set the stage for the most difficult obstacle we encountered in planning our reception, because he gave us list after list after list of people to invite. We were planning to have about seventy people. Our venue couldn't comfortably hold more than 150 anyway, but we wanted it to be more intimate. Dave also has a huge extended family, and suddenly we started getting lists of about ten names at a time from his dad, who wanted us to invite distant relatives Dave had never met. Then, even worse, he started giving us lists of his colleagues he expected us to invite. He never asked if this would be all right with us. Dave called his father and told him we couldn't invite all of these people. His dad's response was, 'Don't worry, it's not like they're going to come, anyway,' and later he'd send another list with more names. By this time the colleagues' list stretched to about forty people. I was ready to blow a gasket! We were paying for the reception ourselves, and we weren't planning to pay for an event with 150 people. Dave called his dad again and told him we couldn't possibly pay for all of these people to attend, and that if he wanted to invite them he would have to pay. That was his dad's cue to blow a gasket! He was furious! In the end, he seriously trimmed down his guest list, but we still ended up with about sixteen extra guests of his at the reception. It was uncomfortable having that many people that neither of us knew. I know there were at least two couples there that we didn't meet, and we still don't know who they were. (For all I know they were professional partygoers who snuck in off the street!) Dave's dad didn't end up paying for these guests— he didn't mention the money issue again, and we decided not to pursue it."

Ever thrown a party? Cast your mind back and recall the planning. Perhaps it was a B-Day of significance, someone's thirtieth or eightieth. Whatever the occasion, chances are if you recall the planning with any degree of accuracy, you will be able to reconstruct at least a certain amount of inevitable consternation over who would be invited. And when it comes to weddings these concerns can become a tangle equaled only by rush hour in Manhattan. Plus the complications may come from all sides. Your inner bride is already telling you something along the lines of "I want a very small, intimate wedding," or conversely, "I want a huge gala." (How many women have you ever heard say, "Oh, I think I want a wedding of indeterminate size where anyone who wants to come is invited?") But whatever your ideal head count is, you can bet someone else has a different plan.

Think like an academic for a second. There's the bride, and then there's "The Other." OK, don't think like an academic, but it all amounts to the same thing. *You* have one set of needs, and "The Other," that is to say the people who are intimates in your wedding experience (now *there's* a nice euphemism) have their needs. Sometimes it's a real challenge to get the twain to meet. Say your mom wants you to invite that distant relation from Timbuktu she admires so much, but you actively dislike. Say your sister feels that her husband's business colleague (the one who gave you that soul-sucking job you took when you were completely desperate) should be invited because otherwise he may take it out on her husband. And on, and on, and nauseatingly on. Any and all of these variants (and many more) pose one of the biggest dangers between Sane You and Going Bridal You.

The Treatment: Lay Down the Law

The Goal: So the majority of guests at your wedding are people that you actually want to celebrate with. (Say, isn't that the point?)

The Application: Realizing that sooner or later you and your LSF must Lay Down the Law is absolutely imperative in any I Think You Should Invite So-and-So scenario. True, if someone else is paying for some portion of your wedding, this may not be possible without high-level negotiations before you get to that point of law-laying. But unless someone is footing the entire bill and has laid prior claim to all control, you gotta be tough as the proverbial nails. Sing all those R-E-S-P-E-C-T songs to get yourself worked up . . . then Lay Down the Law. You might want to consider what Ms. Hannah, she of the intractable dad–in–law, wishes she had done when he started auditioning the cast of thousands for her reception.

"I wish that Dave and I had gone together to talk with his father in person before things got so far out of hand. I think his father tends to ignore anything Dave says that he doesn't want to hear. He would have been shocked to hear the objections coming from me as well. Also, this was a case where meeting face-to-face would have given it a lot more weight than a phone call. You can always hide behind the phone or e-mail, but if we were sitting across from him and clearly stating his guest list was a problem, I really think he would have been forced to deal with the situation. We should have presented a united front on the issue and stood firm."

Ah yes, the united front. The one where you and he must come to an agreement and then Lay Down the Law. Of course not every situation is as extreme as Hannah's. But unless you are having a wedding with literally a few people (you, the guy, and the preacher woman), figuring out who is on your guest list is inherently trying. Especially if you start embracing the insidious concept that your wedding is a place to be as politically correct as possible. That is to say, you start making decisions based not on who you actually *want* to have at your wedding, but based on whom you think you *should* invite. For example: You think you should invite your boss even though you actually despise the guy, because it might up your stock at work. You tell yourself you can't invite your one real friend from work without inviting the other thirty coworkers who might get their collective knickers in a knot, so you don't invite any of them including the one real friend. You think you should invite those distant cousins that everyone in your immediate family thinks of as complete lowlifes, simply because they invited you to one of their weddings in the past decade.

Invitations, Anyone?

You've made the list (whew!), now you need the invites. Consider some anti–Going Bridal advice from a pro, Francine Sperantzas of Oh How Cute, purveyors of wedding invitations.

- Don't forget that even when your invites are printed there can be mistakes to correct—leave enough time!
- Don't forget that something as no-brainer as rounding up addresses and licking stamps actually takes a considerable number of hours, if not days—leave enough time!
- Don't forget that decisions about invitation design are best delivered by one person, not a panicked, squabbling last-minute committee—leave enough time!

This sort of PC invite list thinking can, if you let it, make you Go (Totally) Bridal, because there is never an end to it. Of course it is true that if you can afford it and are so inclined, you may use your wedding as a device to advance your career, pay off old social debts, and so on. But if you hope your wedding will be purely a celebration of the heart, trying to combine this lovely concept with the PC-invitees approach will run you smack into the roadblock of incompatibility. In that case you need to recognize that it's simply not possible to have everyone and their dog's cousin there on The Day. And although there may be consequences, that's true of every decision in life, no? So yes, some people may be miffed, ticked, or otherwise outraged not to have been invited. But since when are you responsible for the emotional state of the entire universe? Make your list, check it twice, and regretfully omit some who are both naughty and nice and then . . . Lay Down the Law.

The Trigger: But It's Only Money

When it comes to wedding-planning logistics, there is one governing factor that must be dealt with. Hopefully before it's presented to you on a maxed-out credit card platter to the tune of "Here Comes the Bill." It's an adjunct to the concerns of Time and Space, largely because it's what pays for the latter. (Not to mention covering other sundry wedding doodads, such as banquets, banks of roses, honeymoons in Paris.) Yes indeedy, money not only makes the world go round, it can also make some women . . . Go Bridal.

Tanya, frugal bride that she was, encountered the financial trigger to the condition as soon as she started to plan. "I got extremely tired of having people tell me I shouldn't let money be such a big issue when I was planning my wedding," says Tanya. "Sometimes I had professionals imply this. For example, a saleswoman in a boutique who looked at me and said, 'But you want to look fabulous, don't you? Aren't you worth it?' when I told her I couldn't afford the dress she was trying to sell me. Other times when I complained to friends about the mounting cost of everything associated with the wedding, they'd tell me I shouldn't worry about it. After all, I was 'only doing it once.' Well sure, that's what I hoped too, but just because I was only doing it once didn't mean I should have to pay for it forever!"

Unless you are very rich (in which case you are probably not reading this book, busy as you are auditioning wedding planners), you know that money, be it the root of all evil or not, can certainly be the route to Going Bridal. And when it comes to weddings, it's all too easy to deny that you are refusing to recognize that your net income is not balancing your gross wedding-spending habits.

There are reams of information available about budgeting for weddings. (Not to mention innocently detailing all the wonderful opportunities you now have to blow all your hard-earned coin.) But how do you respond when it isn't actually your own inner rich princess who's exerting pressure on you to spend, spend, spend? When the pressure to spend, spend, spend comes from the vendors and even friends encouraging you to throw caution to the wind? Resulting in your disappearing greenbacks making you see red, ultimately . . . Going Bridal.

The Treatment: But It's *My* Only Money

The Goal: So that when The Day rolls around you aren't still ignoring those credit card bills amassing beneath the dust bunnies in your hall. (And in the cold light of postwedding reality you're back to drinking beer instead of champagne, but at least you have the dough to pay for the brewskies.)

The Application: This treatment is especially useful in the face of anyone trying to sell you something (the designer gown, the twenty-four-piece swing orchestra, the real champagne as opposed to the baby duck). Because, understandably enough, you don't particularly want to end up in the category of "a fool and her money are soon parted." So while you may engage in much creative thinking as to how you can keep your wedding affordable (say your priest is also a DJ, and is willing to give you a two-for-one-deal, why not?), you may also need to have this treatment at the ready, to be applied at regular intervals. As in, "Yes, it is only money. *My* money, which is finite. Much like this conversation, which I'm afraid is now *finito*." You really do need to know how much money you can spend, and have some idea of your literal and emotional overdraft. And recognize that only you can sign on the dotted line . . . or not. The final analysis? She who is spineless is she who gets stiffed.

"Ms. Bride, We're Ready for Your Close-Up!"

Chances are some of your wedding dollars will go to capturing The Day, via dozens of sticky-fingered disposables or through the viewfinder of a pro. If you go with the latter, consider the following anti–Going Bridal tips offered by Lara Hart of Arrow Productions Photography.

- Try to comparison-shop, but only up to a point—meeting more than about three photogs will likely drive you crazy. Take the time for up close and personal, since meeting in person will give you a sense of the photographer's style. Ask yourself, does he or she seem organized and professional?
- Try to find a photographer whose personality you like as much as his or her work. Think on it—this person will potentially be with you for more hours than some guests on your wedding day. It matters that the photographer cares about what is important to *you*.
- Try to find someone who loves what he or she does and likes weddings—a crime scene photographer does not necessarily a good wedding photographer make!

DIAGNOSING VENDOR-INDUCED GOING BRIDAL: THE SYMPTOMS, THE TRIGGERS, THE TREATMENTS, THE GOALS

Symptoms of Vendor-Induced Going Bridal

- After weeks of negotiations with Hand Printed by Strangers and Son, you finally get your invitations back. Just as you're exiting the shop, "and Son" casually asks if you realize that you're getting married the day the clocks shift to daylight savings time. You wonder if throwing a box of 150 invitations at a total stranger is a federal offense.

- You've chosen a dress off the rack at Hoity Bridal Boutique, rather than going for their incredibly expensive customized gowns. When the alterations prove a tad complicated, the Hoity Bridal Boutique owner says, smugly, "What do you expect when you shop off the rack?" Eureka! You've finally figured out what you want to be when you grow up! An investigative journalist exposing the corruption rampant in some sectors of the wedding industry.

- Your caterer forgets (1) your name, (2) that you're having a vegetarian wedding, and (3) that you're getting married in three months, not six. Then, oddly enough, you decide to (4) forget your caterer. But not before losing both a deposit and your temper, the account of which is told and retold to any passing stranger willing to listen and nod.

- Your hairdresser, who is chronically behind schedule at the best of times, allows as to how she has booked two other brides the same morning as The Day. You realize for the first time what "tearing your hair out" actually refers to.

- You're about to hire a DJ who tells you he totally gets what kind of music you want, claiming his own taste also runs to classical. Then he says, "Of course you'll be wanting the crowd-pleasers, so I'll do my special Macarena, Chicken Dance, YMCA mix—you'll love it." You tell him not only will you not love it, you'll destroy his entire sound system if it comes anywhere near your wedding.

The Trigger: The Dress–Induced Going Bridal

Ah, The Dress. That Dress. Is there any other? Unless you are appearing in Stratford's next production or perhaps at the Met, probably not. Even the most casual, down-dressing, fashion-is-a-capitalist-plot bride is bound to have some concerns about how she wants to appear on The Day. (If not, likely she isn't having The Day.)

Tales of The Dress–Induced Going Bridal are rampant, ranging from sagas of (not) fitting horrors, to epics about dresses ordered in styles that no longer exist as the wedding day approaches, to boutique employees who rudely criticize their clients' weight gains. Thankfully these nightmares are balanced by considerate, talented designers and boutique employees who do fabulous work, on time, with a great deal of regard for their clients' wishes and mental health. But these good women don't make you Go Bridal, and consequently mustn't feel slighted not to be represented in the pages of this book.

Let's turn instead to an account of The Dress–Induced Going Bridal that rings with a dull note of familiarity, the legacy of decades of similar yarns, told by brides who were as irate as was Cory. "I was getting married in May, and started shopping for the dress in January," says Cory. "I originally wanted to buy a dress from a regular dress shop, but I didn't find anything that was right. So I decided to start looking at a few bridal shops. First thing was having my terminology corrected—being told it wasn't a wedding *dress* I wanted, it was a wedding *gown*! Please. But what really drove me crazy was every salesperson would ask when my wedding was, and when I said 'in five months' they would gasp and scold me for being 'so late.' I didn't feel like a client, more like some child reprimanded for not handing in a school assignment on time. Finally I ended up at one boutique where there were a few prospects. Because I didn't have an appointment I had to wait ages for a fitting room. Try sitting in a bridal shop for almost three hours listening to brides-to-be who are fixated on their 'gowns,' totally oblivious to the real world. By the time my turn came, I had selected three dresses and another one off a sale rack. The associate, as I was instructed to call her, proceeded to tell me the one from the sale rack had to be tried on in the self-serve area—basically the dressing rooms around the corner. After pleading she agreed if there was time she would deign to let me try the sale rack dress on. Eventually I picked one of the dresses, and she reluctantly admitted they could put in a rush order. But after waiting in line at the ATM to get cash for the deposit, I was informed there would be a $150 rush fee! I was upset, but what can you do, they know you need a dress. When questioning the fee, I got a lecture on how brides need to order their dresses eight to twelve months in advance and allow another two months for alterations."

Cory's story didn't end there. No, there were unexpected alteration fees, appointments the boutique insisted on scheduling during the middle of her workday, and multiple other irritants. All of which made her . . . Go Bridal.

The Treatment: Talking Yourself Down

The Goal: To end up on your wedding day attired in a way that suits you just fine, thank you very much, whether that be a dress, a gown, a pantsuit, or a Tyrolean goat-herding outfit.

The Application: Deciding what to wear for one's wedding is frequently a case of separating the dresses from the gowns. Consider the following. This is how the *American Heritage Dictionary of the English Language*, fourth edition, defines dress: "A one piece outer garment for women or girls." And this, my friends, is how they define gown: "A long, usually formal dress for a woman." If you embrace the distinction, and the concept of gown seems far superior (appealing to both your sense of glamour and womanhood), then you will likely be shopping in bridal boutiques or chatting up designers. If so, you pretty much have to play by their rules—the rules that drive many a modern, in-a-hurry bride mental. So if you find yourself locked in an emporium of white, scaling the heights of frustration as you discover how the game works, you must

immediately begin to Talk Yourself Down. Perhaps start by reminding yourself that the boutique is not inherently evil—every business has its own particular timetables, bureaucracy, and seemingly
ridiculous conventions. It's just that you, especially if you're a neo-
phyte bride, may be utterly unfamiliar with these rarified codes of
behavior. You may feel that the alteration fees, rush fees, and so on
and so forth are calculated to rob you of your hard-earned dollars.
And in some cases, perhaps they are. But Talk Yourself Down from
your urge to pitch a fit about this miscarriage of justice, by reminding yourself that you do have alternatives. You can, after all, acquire
your finery from any number of alternate sources. (A local dressmaker, your neighborhood "cute frocks for swell chicks" boutique,
your grandmother's attic.) Mind you, it cannot be denied that if you
dream of The Gown, whether it be frothy princess or urban chic,
it will most likely come via a purveyor of bridal accoutrements. So
tread carefully if you have your bridal heart set on something made
by a designer or procured from an official bridal boutique. If you
don't want the experience of obtaining said garment to become the
one part of recalling your wedding that makes you cry—for the
wrong reasons—you'd best consider Cory's post-gown-shopping
reflections, perhaps putting some of her ideas into practice before
any Talking Down is necessary. "Looking back I realize I should
have told them up front that my wedding was small and I was looking for something very simple and within a short time frame, and
not wasted either my time or theirs, or spent more money than I
wanted," says Cory. "Or I might have prepared myself mentally that
I would have to do a lot of sale rack shopping, rather than thinking 'simple' would be easy to find quickly. I definitely would ask up
front, before my heart was set on the dress, what type of rush
charges would be applicable."

Twenty-twenty hindsighted Cory also mentions she could have
just scrapped the whole wedding-specific dress concept entirely, and

returned to her quest to find a dress in one of those most unlikely of hiding places—a dress shop. Which certainly can be less tightly wound locales than your typical bridal boutique, given they are not swarmed by other, similarly anxious brides-in-training. It's also true that one could turn to a talented sewing friend, or the local humble seamstress. But remember, talented sewing friend and local humble seamstress have lives, with their own crises, scheduling issues, and all the rest.

"Anyone Who Says It's Difficult to Find the Right Man Has Never Had to Find the Right Dress."

Designer Catherine Cooper of Urban Bride is fond of the above quote. That said, she believes there's no reason to get into a life-or-death lather over procuring your wedding togs. A few anti–Going Bridal hints from Ms. Cooper:

- Don't forget, you're not looking for that one perfect dress. There are tons of dresses you will look amazing in. Pick a dress you feel like yourself in.
- Don't forget, you're the boss—you can call the shots at the bridal salon, let them know what you do like, don't like, and what you are willing to try out.
- Don't forget, hold back your emotions. Be analytical about the style and cut of the dresses and how they look on your body first. Narrow it down to a couple of favorites, and only then start visualizing your walk down the aisle!

Ultimately it comes down to a question of attitude. You can choose to think your wedding dress is the most significant garb you will ever don, the regalia by which you will always be remembered. Or you can choose to think, "Hey, it's cool to have a great frock that looks pretty damned fine on my wedding day."

The Trigger: Will That Be Chicken or Beef?

When it comes to feeding guests at a wedding, the options are not, surprise, surprise, unlimited. (Not unless your cash is.) There are, of course, weddings where the guests are not served food at all, which may be a reasonable alternative in some cases. Say, for instance, the ceremony is at 2:00 P.M., followed by a quick meet-and-greet, with the invite clearly stating all guests must go by 3:30. But barring this less-than-typical circumstance, generally the bride and groom want to provide some sort of edibles, be they glamorous gourmet fare or down-home grub. This may lead to the age-old issue of buffet versus sit-down; reception hall with catering included versus reception hall without; hors d'oeuvres and starters versus the full meal deal. Many of these weighty decisions will be made on the basis of number of guests and dollars. But even when such matters are settled, there is often another juggernaut ahead: The Menu. Megan is a bride who found that The Menu became her own private hell. "Among my guests there were diabetics, vegetarians, people who were lactose intolerant, vegans, a couple with gluten intolerance, and a few kids who seemed to only eat noodles and ketchup. Obviously I had to abandon my preference of a beautiful sit-down dinner, and go the buffet route. The caterer seemed OK with all this diversity at first, promising there'd be a spread that would cover all of the bases. I thought it was settled. When we finally talked again—I left multiple messages before she got back to me—she told me she wouldn't be able to provide some of the options after all. She did have substitutions, but none of them seemed as good. This just pushed my buttons and made me feel misled. I wanted to cancel with her but I didn't want to fight about the deposit, and I didn't want to go through the hassle of finding someone else."

The Treatment: Word of Mouth

The Goal: So that during the wedding reception you're not anxiously glancing over your shoulder to see if that really is an entire roast suckling pig the waiters are ferrying out to your vegetarian crowd, and not only did the dish run away with the spoon, your entire wedding dinner somehow up and went AWOL.

The Application: Word of Mouth must be applied before you even speak to a potential caterer. This should be relatively simple—asking everyone you know if they've been to some lovely celebration catered by a pro who knew how many servings of champers are in a gallon, returned phone calls, and seemed genuinely pleased to be involved in the event. Not to say that your source will be your soul mate of tastes and preferences. But at the very least you can get a sense of the bottom line via Word of Mouth: is the company reliable, run by people who are polite (they return phone calls!), and cooperative. However, this treatment doesn't stop once you've found The World's Most Superlative Caterer. No, Word of Mouth must be applied in another fashion throughout any contract negotiating, menu planning, place settings proposals, and so on. (Some call this form of the application "a dialogue," still others refer to it as "communication.") You need to feel comfortable asking all your questions ("Remind me again how the Ostrich Tartare is cooked?"), and you should expect to be educated as to the options ("Actually, tents for over six hundred guests do cost extra."). It behooves the bride to remember that neither you nor the folks slinging enchiladas on The Day are mind readers—it's up to you to communicate your questions and concerns. Something menu-challenged Megan pretty much disregarded until she was well into the thick of it. Unfortunately the thick was shared by a caterer who turned out to be playing by her own incomprehensible rules. "Were I to do it again," says Megan, "I would have talked to this woman way more at the very beginning. I didn't really know anything about her, actually, I just picked her off a website. I was pretty casual about it, which was kind of silly when you think how much money we were spending on food—more than on anything else. I think I was also just so grateful when she said her company could take on the complicated menu situation that I didn't feel I should pester her about other details. And at first when she didn't return my calls I just let it ride. Now I wish that once she started ignoring my calls, I'd just bailed. It's not like there's only one game in town, after all."

All Caterers Are Not Created Equal

Beth Vincer of Absolute Catering compares the caterer-client relationship to a partnership—and reminds us that all partnerships are not matches made in heaven. Her anti–Going Bridal advice:

- All caterers are not the same . . . but any caterer worth his or her salt, so to speak, will provide references. Call them!
- All caterers are not the same . . . so remember, Betty Sue catering out of her basement may be cheap, but she may also not be there to refund your deposit when she goes out of business a week before your wedding.
- All caterers are not the same . . . but there's no excuse for the legendary refusal to return phone calls. *You're* not the one who is nuts for expecting a call back in short order.
- All caterers are not the same . . . and a caterer who takes an interest in the potential dynamics at your wedding—the parents who can't sit together, for instance—is your running mate.

"THAT'S BECAUSE IT WAS MADE WITH LOOOVE"

There's no doubt about it, planning can be a real pain in the butt . . . but . . . as any bride knows, it's inescapable—whether it's a wedding brunch for twenty in the in-laws' breakfast nook, or an exotic buffet for two hundred in the Bermuda Triangle. Even when you hire a wedding coordinator, planner, or naive friend for the purposes of keeping the good ship *Wedding* afloat there are still inevitably numerous decisions to be red-stamped; people with differing ideas to be placated; negotiations and (hopefully) collaborations. Still, planning can be (yes, really!) part of the fun. Consider this—in choosing the faux-ermine trim over the real fur on your train, the carpaccio over the tofu dogs, the backdrop mural of Paris rather than the more expensive location along the Seine, you (and possibly your fiancé) are designing an event/party/ritual that is an expression of the pair of you. If you wear that notion lightly, it may help during the moments that seem less about any sort of vision and more about making sure there are adequate supplies of wet naps. Although your wedding day is (thankfully) not Andrew Lloyd Webber material, like any other festivity/celebration/ceremony it does require forethought, effort, and creativity. Thus the end result can be, should you choose to look at it this way, a reflection of the passion, love, and joy that was put into its creation.

Try on this analogy. Ever experienced that hammy moment when a friend dishes out her very own special spaghetti sauce and in response to your appreciation says, "That's because it was made with looove"? As corny as it is, there's truth in it. You may not wish to equate your wedding with pasta sauce, point taken. Nonetheless, weddings that are fashioned with looove (in between hair-tearing-out moments) tend to have a wonderful spirit, tangible to all who are present. And a celebration of love from start through planning to finish is truly a wedding to remember.

6

Oh Yeah, Whatshisname

A Tale of It Takes Two Not to Tango, as Told by the Bride

Maybe he's not so long-suffering. At least, that was my thought tonight after I came home and freaked (yes, I admit it, *freaked*!) about the fact that the wedding is a month away, and we still don't have certain details in hand. Details such as some kind of cake, some kind of photographer, and some kind of outfit he's planning to wear that isn't jeans and a T-shirt.

Typically whenever I've had the odd wedding woe, my Long-Suffering Fiancé has certainly lived up to the nickname. A veritable Mr. "Everything Will Be All Right, You'll See." And perhaps, much as it pains me to admit it, I've been taking his fabulously unflappable attitude for granted. (Certainly *he* believes this to be the case.) But lately I've also started thinking that maybe his abnormally high quotient of "don't worry, be happy" is partly some subliminal form of avoidance. OK, call me an armchair psychoanalyst, but don't you think there's something a little strange about a guy who's perpetually perky?

This suspicion was confirmed when I came home to a voice mail filled with the following: The reception site manager saying they're no longer doing cakes, and why did we leave it until so late anyway? My pal Priya, back from elopement, all chipper about a friend of a friend who takes decent snapshots and is eager to do so for our wedding, as long as we make sure he has a constant supply of wine. My dressmaker, whispering nervously into the phone that she thinks there's a bit of a problem with the shawl—no big deal, just that the fabric has gone AWOL. My mother, suggesting we meet tomorrow during my workday to finalize details of the order of ceremony (although no such order has been established), with a postscript suggesting that my sister may not be speaking to me if I don't call her tonight. And dear friend Angela, in tears because her betrothed (Dog Boy, remember him?) is now saying he wants to postpone.

Frantically scribbling down the messages with a dull pencil (LSF *never* leaves the pen by the phone), I could feel something akin to PMS meets bad hair day times ten threatening to erupt. I swear my entire body temperature must have shot up five degrees! So *this* is wedding fever, my addled brain told me, clearly an attempt to restore my usual black sense of humor. No takers—I was still furious with The Wedding. And then when my darling affianced heard me fuming about the content of the calls (which he himself had listened to earlier but failed to notate), all he had to say was, "Hey babe, don't worry, everything will work out just fine." Oddly enough, this time it wasn't soothing. This time it was maddening. So much so that I shrieked, "No! No! It won't be fine! In fact it's totally f*@#d! Why am I the only one who's concerned about the details? And why must you be so eternally optimistic—don't you know how totally annoying that is?"

I saw a look steal o'er his visage I can only describe as a "last straw" look. Followed by a definite downshift in optimism.

"OK," he said, "I've been trying my best to be supportive, sensitive, a good listener. I've been working on the friggin' To-Do List." (Here he waved his half of the list, without, I noticed, a great deal checked off.) "But it takes two to tango, right? This was supposed to be fun, right? And now you're telling me you're mad because I'm too positive and I don't see the point in needlessly worrying about the details? That's just not right, right?"

And with that he stomped to the door, muttering something about going for a run or a beer or maybe both, I didn't really listen. No, I was too busy snapping the damned pencil in half.

Memo to Self: Celebration of Two, Not One

It is one of life's greater ironies that the quintessential celebration of two, a.k.a. a wedding, can also be the very thing that makes the two in question feel that they are sometimes at opposite ends of the same playing field. And although there are (so they say) many couples who happily plan their weddings without a shred of disagreement, others find it to be a somewhat stressful time during the course of their lives together. (News flash: UNDERSTATEMENT.) This may be most severe in situations where it is implicit (or explicit) that the whole durn "wedding in white" is really about . . . The Bride. A notion reinforced by reams of empirical evidence indicating that women tend to invest themselves, both emotionally and pragmatically, to a more extreme degree in their wedding planning than do their fiancés.

But just because this book (and perhaps most weddings) are bridecentric doesn't mean *your* wedding has to follow suit. It also doesn't mean you have to adhere to the unhealthy practice of putting your fiancé (and thereby your relationship) on hold during wedding planning. After all, the issues that will be raised time and time again during the course of your marriage are likely going to be present in the weeks and months leading up to The Big Day. For example: spending habits versus saving habits; attention to details versus the big picture; spontaneous decision making versus careful consideration of options; sex versus not . . . In other words, any differences or issues that may crop up during normal life (that sweet calm world that exists when you're *not* planning a wedding) can become heightened cartoon versions during the buildup to W-Day. No surprise, given wedding planning is a condensed course in decision making under duress.

It may prove helpful to remind yourself and your beau that the wedding really is a celebration of two, not one. It may prove essential to recall that the planning of it might (or might not) interest you more than it will him. Any scenario is possible. You could divvy up the work equitably and proceed with good cheer. (Yay!) Or you could not, quarrelling furiously over the division of labor. (Boo!) You could agree to do the initial organizing, he the follow-up, and everything is fine . . . or not. You might acknowledge that planning the wedding actually does matter more to one of you, and accept that the "passionate-about-weddings" member of your party will happily take on the lioness's share. Or you might come to this conclusion only to find that several months later the person shouldering that load is smoldering with resentment.

Of course it is possible (though not probable) that you may be so lucky as to never ever have your beloved cause you any Going Bridal moments, regardless of the intensity (or lack thereof) of his involvement. But let's suppose for a hypothetical second (or for most of the rest of the chapter) otherwise. Let's assume you are one of the brides-to-be who does find the dynamic between you and your intended a mite challenging, at least on occasion.

Indeed, let us be frank: as fond as you are of the guy, he's driving you stark raving.

THE SANITY-ROBBER BRIDEGROOM

What could cause this? Usually, it's the extremes. Say the gentleman in question unilaterally decides to bow out of the process, possibly only reappearing to repeat irksome phrases such as "Whatever you want is fine with me as long as it doesn't cost over five hundred dollars." Conversely, there are some cases where the groom via his enthusiastic embrace of the event ensures that he is constantly, nose-pokingly present, challenging your every wedding-related thought. Either scenario, naturally enough, might cause you to . . . Go Bridal. However, your groom may not embody one of the spiky ends of the spectrum. It's possible your mister's ability to trigger your Going Bridal tendencies may simply arise because he just didn't bargain for how much additional stress wedding planning would introduce into your already busy lives. Particularly where it concerns his beloved. He may suddenly feel as though the normal demands on your time— your omnipresent career, your omnivorous family commitments and, why, your old future husband himself—are somehow second-class citizens. That the only dignitary of note is The Wedding, a creature that must constantly be appeased. Whereas you may feel you are the only creature doing the appeasing—to groom, family, career, and of course, to the wedding. No wonder the two of you might get a little snippy with each other!

So what would be ideal? That there is consensus. That you can have a mutually acceptable strategy for getting from that moment of "yes" to the moment of "I do." That you both realize the strategy emerges from a process. And that the process requires regular communication to move it out of any slough of wedding-planning despair. That you are partners, recognizing and playing to each other's strengths. (And that you are not totally bitchy about his weaknesses.)

He Said, She Said

Interestingly enough, some recent brides and grooms have differing views as to how they handled their wedding planning. One may have a version the other might call "revisionist." To wit: recently married couple Alexander and Marina responded (independently, without being privy to the other's thoughts) to the following miniquestionnaire in such a way that this tendency is clearly revealed.

Q: What did you like least about planning your wedding with your betrothed?

He Said: "I really got tired of all the low-key tension between Marina and my family members about how things were going to be. A good friend of mine put it most clearly. 'The groom's job,' he said, 'is to put out the fires.' That's how it felt at times, being the fire chief between Marina and the rest of the world."

She Said: "Getting all the details into perspective on my own was hard enough. But then I had to negotiate everyone's wishes, mine, my in-laws, and Alex's. He didn't always understand what the differences were about, nor was he always terribly proactive. He just wanted everyone to get along."

(Editorial comment: Hmm . . . did you guys plan the same wedding?)

Q: Who do you think did most of the work re planning your wedding?

He Said: "I'd say I did a bit more, although for sure Marina paid far more attention to the little details. But I dealt with all the vendors and contracts and the major things like that."

She Said: "Definitely me, I was on it day in day out. To be fair, Alexander handled stuff like signing off on contracts. But that was after I'd already sussed out the options."

(Editorial comment: In case you needed proof that there really *are* two sides to every story.)

Q: Do men or women get more riled up about wedding planning in general?

He Said: "It's a bigger deal for the bride. I hate saying that because it sounds sexist and old-fashioned, but many women have a set opinion about what their 'special day' will be like. And God help you if you stand in their way!"

She Said: "It's not always women who get worked up, though I'd say nine times out of ten it is. But often that's because women recognize the subtleties involved, and they understand how much energy the whole thing takes. I think there are still lots of men who even in this day and age think it's ultimately just about showing up on the day and saying, 'I do.' Incredible! But true."

(Editorial sound effect: cymbal crash.)

DIAGNOSING GROOM-INDUCED GOING BRIDAL: THE SYMPTOMS, THE TRIGGERS, THE TREATMENTS, THE GOALS

Symptoms of Groom-Induced Going Bridal

- You ask your betrothed what he thinks of the cake idea, the table centerpiece idea, the hors d'oeuvres idea—basically the anything-and-everything-connected-with-the-reception idea —and when he issues his standard response, "Whatever you like, honey," you discover what the phrase "He's driving me crazy" actually means. (As you speed-dial your therapist.)
- He gets so gleefully caught up in all things Wedding that he barrages you with e-mails about every detail right down to his preferences regarding the bridesmaids' shoes. You find yourself panicking, "Holy shit, I'm marrying my best girlfriend!"

- You've always known he tends to procrastinate, but when a week away from the wedding he still hasn't "gotten around" to dropping into the tux rental joint, you tell him that's fine, since you've decided the wedding is going to be "dry" (as in no booze), which will offset those last-minute tux rental costs.

- Your intended claims (against all evidence to the contrary) not to be a cheapskate, but when he tells you he thinks the reception shouldn't cost more than eight bucks a head, you present him with a menu plan that goes like this: starter—iceberg lettuce with vinegar dressing; main—spaghetti with tomato sauce; dessert—animal crackers with water.

- You want to elope, he wants a big shindig, and while still negotiating some middle-ground compromise you discover he's told "just a few people" that it will be a big spring wedding. You tell him it may be a small spring funeral.

- After practically having to tie him down to talk about the wedding, you finally agree on the wording of the invites, the location of the postwedding party, the complex menu plan geared toward your lactose-, wheat-, and meat-intolerant guests. Then he comes out with, "Man, it's such a hassle. Maybe we just shouldn't bother getting married." And you think, "God, I can't wait to start dating again."

The Trigger: Fiancé Knows Best

Let's turn the stage over to Julia, who can enlighten us as to the nature of this trigger to Going Bridal with one surefire example. "My fiancé and I agreed I would do most of the wedding planning. Partly because he's in grad school and working at the same time, partly because I refused to have a long lead-up to the wedding, which is what he wanted. I said I'd take care of most of the organizing since it was happening sooner than he'd like. But whenever I'd fill him in on the details of something I thought we'd agreed on, he would suddenly say it wasn't right. The invitations, for example—my mom and I spent a week figuring them out, I e-mailed it to him, he said fine. Then while we were actually making the template for the invite, he stuck his nose in and said, 'I don't think that sounds right.' This was at the point where we didn't have time to be nit-picking over the wording. I flipped!"

Just to set the record straight, it's not father who knows best. It's you who knows best. And you. And you. And you. Oh yes, we each believe we are reasonable, open-minded, flexible, and otherwise mature in our ability to compromise. But at the same time, deep down, secretly, we know that we, more than anyone else involved, know best. And when it comes to your fiancé, and a gradual recognition that you and he may have vastly differing notions about anything to do with your wedding, hold onto your veil, sister, you're in for a ride.

The Treatment: Put Your Proverbial Cards on the Table . . . and Compromise

The Goal: So by the time you are married you are filled with a greater sense of understanding of each other, as opposed to a greater sense of resentment of each other. (And so that you can begin the marriage-long process of balancing both of your individual needs and desires.)

The Application: Take a long look at yourself. Then take a long look at your fiancé. You are not one. You will never be one. Marriage is essentially the coming together of two entirely different people. (OK, so maybe you both love it when the Jays whip the Yankees' butts, or you both savor Cheese Whiz–garnished martinis, but otherwise? Totally different.)

It's a fact that a great deal of the time you and your betrothed will have different desires, motives, and perceptions. Sadly, one of the biggest crimes of being raised to be "polite" is our general inability to voice those differences directly and kindly. All too quickly it becomes hot-under-the-collar confrontation, or else turns into simmering, brooding silence. No acceptable compromise is reached, because everyone's too busy nursing his or her own particular grievance. But when it comes to wedding planning, reaching compromise (after compromise) is often the only solution to not killing each other. Consequently you both need to put forward, clearly and one would hope without obvious rancor, what each of you wants and needs. (It's nice if you can distinguish between the two.)

Take Julia, for example. She began to feel that she was something of the scullery maid to her own wedding. This bugged her. But for a long time she merely stewed. Then she talked her way out of the servant's quarters. "Since my fiancé had agreed to rush the wedding against his wishes I felt I shouldn't complain about how he responded to the planning. But it was driving me crazy that he kept changing his mind about what he liked and didn't like every time I'd report back with some update. Finally, after hitting bottom with my own feelings about it one night, I just told him how the process was making me feel. I was pretty calm, and careful not to sound like I was attacking him. When he realized how the process was making me feel, he felt really bad. But talking about it very frankly helped us find a new way of working—we ended up agreeing that before I finalized anything to do with the wedding from then on, we'd both say how we felt about it, I'd take care of it, and then he'd have to live with the results—without coming back with the last-minute demands. It made it a lot less pressurized."

You rock, Julia.

The Trigger: We Have All the Time in the World

Think about it. If you want to get married tomorrow, you probably can. (If city hall is open, and neither of you is still legally hitched to someone else.) But if you want to get married with a wedding—say some sort of slightly more elaborate ceremony, perhaps including a posy or two and a few loved ones hanging about—it does require a little lag time in between the decision and the "I do." That said, there are some grooms who feel that time is far more elastic than it appears to some brides. For instance Rachel, who says her groom participated in about 20 percent of the planning ("talking about ideas and researching options wasn't for him") and about 80 percent of the organizing ("he was in on final decisions about everything"). Regardless of his P&O (planning and organizing) percentile, it seems Rachel's man has consistently viewed the process as occurring on a different timeline than has his lovely fiancée. "We're seven weeks away from our wedding," says Rachel. "And last night we went out with our groomsmen only to find out that neither of them have finalized their outfits. My fiancé couldn't seem to understand my concern about this. To me, seven weeks is a blink of an eye, to my fiancé it's a lifetime. Yeah, you could say this is causing a 'bit' of stress."

Time, its passage, and how it is viewed differently by some men and some women underlies many a tension betwixt bride and groom. You may have to find ways to convey your perspective of that ticking clock in terms that your betrothed will clearly understand. For instance, "Seven and a half weeks sounds like forever, it's true. But if you subtract all the workdays, plus the evenings we've already booked for socializing and such, why this leaves us seven and a half *days* left to plan the wedding." Or, "Seven weeks, about three weeks shy of the remainder of the baseball season after the all-star break—yes, *that* short!"

The Treatment: Please Just Do It for Me
The Goal: So that you do not end up becoming a stereotype before you're even married. (Not that you aspire to either designation, but it's supposed to be the nagging *wife*, not the nagging *bride*.) And so

that you can both achieve some peace of mind, while in the P&O midst.

The Application: You know how it goes. You think something's the end of the world as you know it, and he says, "Don't worry, it'll all work out." Or you think he's being obsessively childish about some altercation; he's irked that you don't realize its significance. There are volumes written about the differing interpretations of the same situation by men versus women, with theories both social and biological as to why this is so. (And yes, there are strenuous deniers who insist this is pure stereotyping, clichéd and untrue—but they don't get out much.) It should come as no surprise that in the throes of wedding planning some of these gender-oriented differences in interpreting matters both large and small may come to the fore. This can lead to occasions where you feel very strongly about a particular situation, but you know that although he views it in an entirely different light, it ultimately matters not a jot to him. In such cases you may have to apply the old "Please Just Do It for Me."

Talk Like a Tactician, Volume 1

- Perhaps you feel the centerpiece's red anthuriums absolutely must be interwoven with glossy liguaria leaves for full effect, based on a gorgeous display you once saw in New Zealand; perhaps he's less passionate about floral theater. Perhaps ultimately you are both allowed to feel the way you feel?

- Perhaps instead of graciously allowing him to put stamps on the invitations (or granting him any number of other menial tasks), graciously consider his opinions on the significant matters, lest he get cranky, and you . . . Go Bridal.

- Perhaps when he tells you he thinks you've "gone off your nut" over the wedding, instead of shouting, "No wonder, with you saying incredibly insensitive things like that," you might suggest you need his patience even more than his perceptions.

Some hard-nosers see this treatment as manipulative. Phooey on them. Yes, it's not optimum—best would be a mature negotiation leading to mutually acceptable accordance. But this is real life, where it's possible to talk until you're blue in the face and still not share the vision. So it doesn't mean it's dishonest to ask your beloved to "Please Just Do It for Me." It's merely acknowledging that there are circumstances in which you and your spousal-unit-to-be don't see eye to eye, and it behooves said unit to simply do you the favor of acquiescing to your wishes. Why? Because he loves you and understands it will make you feel better. And heck, you may even do the same for him one fine day.

The Trigger: Too Little Information

In the so-called "information age" there's a constant low-level rumble of potential overload, whether it's caused by trying to interpret contradictory reports about world-altering crises, or by sorting through trivial (but compelling) updates on what the beautiful people are doing. So much to read about, so little time. When it comes to weddings, the detail bombardment can drive you to distraction (or at least to too many evenings spent vegging in front of the TV, wine glass in hand, desperately trying not to have a wedding panic attack).

It has been noted that in certain discrete cases some grooms are particularly unreceptive to the aforementioned wealth of wedding details. Bride Lata has this to say about that: "From the beginning our wedding plans were complicated because of cultural differences—my family is originally from India, his family is French. We were having a Hindu ceremony and a Christian ceremony on the same day. As if that wasn't enough to make me crazy, I discovered as we started to plan that he was very resistant to hearing about the details. He seemed to expect me and my family to make all the decisions. But I felt strongly it was a partnership—the expression 'start as you mean to go on' applied. It all blew up over the wedding feast.

Early on I suggested we bypass cuisine from either of our cultures, and go with something else, like Italian. When it came time to actually make choices and decisions about this, his response was, 'But we already talked about it, we don't need to talk about it again, do we?' This was about the tenth time in a row he said something like this, and I blew my top."

The Treatment: I Now Call This Meeting to Order

The Goal: To come to the understanding that although you may have different orbits around Planet Wedding, you really do both want to end up happily married here on earth.

The Application: Recall for a minute, if you will, that quaint saying about the word "assume." You know the one: "It makes an ass out of u and me?" Sadly, this often applies during the wedding-planning marathon. Lata, for example, admits she was so fixated on the potentially exasperating cross-cultural nature of her wedding that she just assumed her betrothed would be as concerned. She assumed he would be an equal partner in sorting it out. He, as it turned out, assumed otherwise. But not before many a slightly ill-conceived and possibly hurtful phrase was bandied about. "I was so frustrated with him, I just nagged and scolded, and he withdrew more and more. Finally he said, 'Look, I really just don't care about this stuff. But I don't want you to be so miserable, what can I do?' I devised a plan that we would meet once a week and sit down for an hour to talk just about the wedding. I called them committee meetings. I'd present all the ideas I'd thought about that week, he could offer his responses, and then I'd go back to planning. This helped enormously, because he knew he had to focus on it at that time, and he did. And he knew I wouldn't constantly be asking his opinions in between meetings. Not a full partnership, but better than what went on before."

Talk Like a Tactician, Volume 2

- Perhaps instead of saying, "Hey buddy, what's with the tiny attention span," you might try, "Dear heart, I'd really appreciate it if we could speak more fully on this subject—you know which one."

- Perhaps instead of saying, "You want something called a 'groom's cake' in the shape of a hockey stick? You're totally kidding me, right?" you might say, "Is it truly important to you to have more than one cake given our budget limitations? And if so, is a sporting theme of the essence?"

- Perhaps instead of saying, "All you can think about is the booze and we haven't even decided on the guest list yet!" you could venture, "I understand you care greatly about the wine vintages, but it would be nice to decide how many of the old folks we actually want to have there to drink them."

The Trigger: The Groom Who Knew Too Much

There are women who dismiss the idea of this sort of groom with a "get real" toss of their bridal locks, but that's simply because they haven't been exposed to grooms who are more invested in planning their weddings than are their brides. But they do exist. And sometimes their existence is indeed a blessing. Say for instance you're completing your Ph.D. and running a restaurant at the same time— why wouldn't you be grateful if he takes on the legwork? Or say you're one of the Lazy Bride tribe, and the idea of planning a party involving more than five people makes you want to pull the covers over your head. Or supposing you recognize that he has totally amazing taste and boundless enthusiasm about all things Wedding, whereas you are concerned with one key matter—The Dress.

On the other hand, there are instances where the hyper-informed, hardest-working groom in wedding business can turn into The Groom Who Knew Too Much. Sheri walked right into this, eyes shut. "My fiancé was very keen to be totally involved in the wedding and I figured, hey, it's his wedding and his money too. What could be wrong with him wanting to do so much? At first it seemed great—he was tireless about researching and calling places. But as we went along, I felt he became involved with things I'd rather he didn't—vetoing the number of bridesmaids, for example. Also I really think he began to withhold information from me, stuff he figured would make me want something different from what he'd decided. He had so much information about the options he could just say—'Look, I've sussed it out, believe me this is the best one.' He basically took over, and at a certain point I felt he was acting like a clichéd wedding-obsessed bride!"

The Treatment: Demanding Full Disclosure

Perhaps you think this treatment will only need to be applied infrequently, say, once a century or so. But you'd be surprised at just how many control freaks, whoops, "extremely detail-oriented people" there are in the universe. Including some grooms. Sheri's frustration with her wedding-obsessed fellow became more acute as they got into issues dearest to her heart. She wanted all six bridesmaids, thank you very much. And she wanted to know just why her idea of a romantic picnic luncheon was so unreasonable when they were, after all, getting married close to a park with a beautiful grove complete with adorable picnic shelters. Finally she demanded full disclosure. "I waited until we were in a calm, private situation with each other, and then told him that I felt that he had made certain decisions regarding the wedding that I wasn't comfortable with. I didn't fully understand why he felt those decisions were so set in stone. I told him I really needed to know all of the thinking behind his decision making, not just be told, 'Don't worry, I've checked out the options, this one is best.' At first he was kind of defensive, saying he wasn't keeping anything back. But eventually it all came out, his reasoning for the choices he'd made. He thought that six bridesmaids would look silly, too cluttered. He didn't think I needed to have two of these women, whom he viewed as less than close friends of mine. He thought eating outside at picnic tables seemed a little déclassé. He was worried about whether we could pull that off and still have a sense of elegance and occasion. Also, a lot of the differences we had over details were about him being more concerned than I was about the way the wedding looked—the style of the wedding. (Maybe the fact that he is a movie set designer has something to do with this!) I told him my reasons for wanting to have all six women, and my feeling that it was more important we have a fun day than some streamlined 'wedding beautiful.' By this point in time we didn't have that much left to decide anyway, and some things were done deals. But we did change a few key things, and he was more open about sharing the information he gathered for whatever remained to be done."

One Small Step for Groom?

- The gradual shift away from "bridal registry" to "wedding" or "gift" registry possibly indicates that the wedding industry sees profit in cautiously promoting the idea that maybe it's *not* just "The Bride's Day."
- The inception of co-ed wedding showers and joint stag/ettes possibly indicates that some members of the erotic entertainment industry may have to find new avenues of employment.
- The inclusion on daytime talk TV of panels of grooms who get overly obsessive about their weddings possibly indicates a dearth of more gripping subject matter.
- A rash of newspaper articles appearing in June with headlines such as "Here Comes the Groom" possibly indicates someone in editorial is covertly watching daytime TV.

By the way, Sheri and her husband (not to mention all six brides-maids) enjoyed a beautiful catered picnic luncheon after their wedding.

Once Upon a Time

Once upon a time . . . there was a great New York ball club called the Brooklyn Dodgers. (Then they moved to L.A., and life was never the same.) Guess what those selfsame Dodgers were originally called, back in 1884? The Brooklyn Bridegrooms. Yup, it's true. Seven of their star players had gotten married at around the same time, and some wise guy came up with the swell name. Thing is, some men are damn proud to be a groom! As well they should be. And yet, if you've been reading the other chapters of this book, or any other wedding-related treatise for that matter, you might not know it. You might think, for example, that in the final analysis weddings are the business of wives-to-be, and those über-involved grooms mentioned above are some sort of whimsical aberration. It seems only fair then that we should allow at least a portion of this book (one or two paragraphs out of two hundred plus pages isn't too much to graciously accede, is it?) to the male half of the equation. Ladies and Gentleman (there's got to be *one* guy reading this), allow me to present . . . The Groom.

I'm Part of This Too!

Sean is an event promoter who describes his wedding as "the hardest gig I've ever booked." That said, he was thrilled to participate fully in planning his wedding, and was frustrated by the reactions he got to his degree of involvement. "Weddings have evolved in our time to be ultimately about the woman. I think this is totally bizarre. Don't get me wrong, I wanted our wedding day to be very special for my fiancée. But I also wanted to be able to experience all of that buildup and excitement too. I wanted the wedding to be a reflection of both of us—there was no way I wasn't going to be able to express myself through my wedding. I made sure I had complete input."

So where was the problem?

"When we were engaged we were living in two different states. And any time I'd sign up for some mailing involving weddings, putting down both of our addresses, the info would go to her. Or when I'd do some preliminary work on something to do with the wedding, the person at the other end of the line would ask when they could speak to my fiancée, to make sure they had all the details right. Frankly, it pissed me off. It made me feel like shouting, 'Hey, I'm part of this too!'"

Sean, you'll be pleased to hear, did *not* make his fiancée, Hilary, Go Bridal. But inadvertently his intensity about their wedding turned out to be instrumental in her family conducting her down that bumpy bridal path.

The Trigger: They All Say He's a Flake

"Sean was passionate about our wedding, and I liked that," says Hilary. "There was a fair bit of stuff to work out with the families, different religious backgrounds being a biggie. He was far better at that than I was—especially with my family, where he kind of ran interference. But it amazed me how deeply resistant people were to his degree of involvement in the details. Our caterer was always looking to me in meetings, as though I was somehow the keeper of the power over whether or not we would have goat cheese canapés or whatever. It was embarrassing. But the worst thing was a couple of my older relatives making snide comments about the groom acting like he was the bride. This just made me furious."

The Treatment: Grin and Bear It

The Goal: So that the worst aspects of conservatism, tradition, and convention that manifest themselves in this get-a-life behavior are kept in their appropriate place—at a distance.

The Application: The great thing about this trigger is that you and your man are united against it. Two against the world, hand in hand defeating all opposition, a veritable Hepburn and Tracy, yada yada yada. This gives you a tremendous amount of cumulative power. But it may be more difficult when you are a lone bride flying solo, facing those irritating gadflies. Here's Hilary: "The thing was, when my relatives would make these comments it was always when Sean wasn't around. I'd tell them about something he'd looked into for the wedding, and they'd snicker and say something stupid about him. And I'd be so mad I'd stomp out, which usually meant my mother was running after me. Eventually Sean convinced me I really had to act like it didn't matter, just smile and think about the wedding and our relationship. And that's what I started to do—tune out. I got quite good at it."

THE FRONT PAGE CHALLENGE

Grin and Bear It can be seen as a handy, catchall ultimate treatment for many of the triggers to Going Bridal. It's not simple to achieve, but the principle is straightforward—focus on what matters to you in the long run, and tune out of the wedding-related static that surrounds you. Furthermore, it's also a skill that could come in handy in the postwedding years to come. Supposing, for example, you're planning to raise a flock of children and Jack Russell terriers in the confines of a small suburban house. Or supposing you intend to pull off your Pulitzer prize–winning journalistic effort while working double shifts at your local TV station's newsroom. Whatever the case may be, there's a lot to be said for focus. For recalling (possibly again and again) that you're getting married because you love the guy. And that whatever happens en route to the wedding (including, potentially, a little white noise from the man himself) is ultimately a sidebar to the front page of your lives together—the marriage.

7

THE BIG DAY, NOT THE HAPPIEST DAY

A TALE OF WEDDING WILLIES, AS TOLD BY THE BRIDE

W-DAY LOOMS, AND I FEAR I've fallen into some very bad pre-game habits. Not too much eating going on, for example. Anxiety, not some sudden acquisition of willpower, has finally caused the five extra pounds I've supposedly been losing since reaching the age of majority to finally slip away. Then there are my increasingly frequent Wedding Day Gone Wrong dreams. There's the one where I'm marrying Dog Boy and screaming "Please, no!" Or the one where I've somehow managed to put on a hideous black workout bra under my wedding dress; it's clearly visible and sends me into such a frenzy I announce to all the assembled guests that I'm going home to change. But just at that point it dawns on me that I actually don't recognize any of these people! My wedding guests are complete strangers, because whoops, I've scheduled the wedding on the wrong day. Let's just say I've become very familiar with the sensation of waking in a puddle of cold sweat.

Even more ridiculous is my sudden (morbid?) interest in Cinderella-meets-Princess-Bride weddings. I find myself compulsively reading about other brides' "special days" (gag) on wedding websites, the smug diaries illustrated with fabulous photographs which probably set someone's daddy back more than our entire wedding budget.

These perfect wedding days always end with the golden couple flitting off to "a private island retreat in Bora Bora" or "the bride's parents' chateau in the Loire Valley" for their honeymoon. And not once in the rundown of the events of The Day do they mention the slightest glitch—say the bride got into a snit with her best friend because said bride's expensive Italian hose ran (and friend forgot to bring the second pair). Or the bride's mother-in-law almost didn't show up because of the humongous fight they'd had the day before. (Sorry Edie, had to tell.) No, it's all "talented sister sang Ave Maria so flawlessly every guest wept," or "bride realizes childhood dream of marrying where the waters of the Atlantic and Pacific merge; guests were suitably attired in penguin suits." No one ever commits a colossal boo-boo, says something unforgivable, forgets to look beautiful or, God help us, fails to thrill to every blessed second of "the happiest day."

Reading these accounts is a bit like another guilty pleasure, romantic pulp fiction. No matter how many you skim through it's always the same too-good-to-be-true conclusion. (Only difference being the guy is called "Rip" instead of "Cash." Imagine, if you will, our hero being named "Bubba.") Anyway, each description of another flawless wedding makes me click and read the next, the Internet equivalent of potato chips. No surprise, when I finally stop I feel queasy.

Realistically I know these preoccupations are probably manifestations of anxiety (please don't tell me you were thinking ". . . of a sick mind"). It's like I'm in the grips of the most prolonged anxiety attack imaginable. Over just about everything: Does forty percent probability of precipitation mean sixty percent rules, or the other way around? Does Ecstatic Edibles really get it that my soon-to-be-husband's entire allergic family will break out in hives if there is so much as a "dash" of real chocolate in that faux mocha icing recipe? Will the lavish lily baskets actually be lavish . . . or limp? Will they arrive on time, or will they be as late as I dread the best man will be, given his scheduled arrival three days prior to the wedding . . . (not) direct from Timbuktu? ("Don't worry," he e-mailed, "the flights are rarely more than a day behind schedule.") And now that I've some-how managed to turn my "intimate prewedding gathering" into a girly fest numbering fifteen (including two gals rumored not to be speaking), will the supposed primping, reminiscing, and otherwise sweetness and light turn into some kind of frenzied hysteria where I'm so wound up I start to cry—*before* the wedding? And, and, and . . . well really, the list of potentially anxiety-provoking issues truly is endless.

Which makes a nice pairing with guilt. ("Why oh why didn't I organize this thing sooner, like they all said I should?!") But every now and then, praises be, there's the proverbial ray of sunshine and I get a glimpse of something beyond a series of potential catastrophes. Instead I see myself and LSF, hand in hand, tears standing in our eyes (or grinning like fools). I see my family and dear friends (and yeah, one or two complete strangers) all gathered together. The toasts being made; the champers being spilled; the musicians playing too loudly; the kids playing, period (and annoying the adults); my single friends blatantly scouting for possibilities; my coupled friends getting all wedding-struck. . . .What I see is The Wedding, careen-ing through the afternoon, unfolding as it will. And me not caring about the discovery of yet another unasked-for "tweak" to the menu, or whether having our first dance to Tuvan throat singing confuses some of the guests. Not getting pissed off when my aunt says, as she almost certainly will, "Well dear, it really was an 'inter-esting' wedding. You *are* happy, aren't you?"

Funnily enough, this is pretty much how it goes on The Day—only just as Auntie is launching her missile, Edie, Angela, and Priya whisk me away for a group bridal moment. Well, all of us freshly bridal except for Angie, who finally turned the tables on Dog Boy, saying he may have postponed the wedding, but she was postponing the relationship—permanently. She's doing the right thing and knows it, and I know most of those tears in her eyes are of happiness—for me. It sends me straight into weepy-love-you-you're-such-a-good-friend-mode, and just when we're both about to totally dissolve I catch my husband's eye ("husband!") across the room, sending me a look of such love I know I'll remember it even when we're a-settin' and a-rockin'.

Just at that moment the sixty percent wins out and it starts to bucket rain. So I throw my skirt up over one elbow and polka my way back inside, family and friends following, wet and laughing. With something that feels like sheer nutty happiness I realize I'm finally letting the wedding do exactly what it's been itching to do since we began Operation Planning and Organizing—have a life all of its own.

IT'S TAKEN ON A LIFE OF ITS OWN

Many a bride has uttered the above phrase about her wedding, and not always happily. Sometimes it's tinged with a shadow of bewilderment, if not outright resentment. After all, how *does* something that is a reasonably small event (in the grand scheme of things) become such a devilishly hot potato? How does it get from being a few scrawls on a pad of paper to taking on the energy of a desperate slippery eel, one end disappearing as soon as the other end is grabbed? You may not like to think of your wedding as a root vegetable or a fish—fair enough. But you get the point. What you thought was a matter of expressing shared values, champagne, thoughtful words, champagne, and deep meaningful statements of love turns out to be "my wedding, the one that got away." In other words, at some point during wedding planning you feel like the whole thing is utterly beyond your ability to truly control.

Why, you may ask, and again, why? The answer lies in the unpredictable nature of people, specifically those involved in your wedding, all with their own agendas and needs. The combined force of all the cooks in the wedding kitchen means, ultimately, that weddings do in fact take on a life of their own—the lives of everyone invested, psychologically, financially, emotionally. Who knew?

Now you do. And it's possible, should you put your mind to it, to turn that little bit of knowledge not into something dangerous, but into something useful. You may want to even go so far as to draw a parallel between the way you feel about the most beloved people in your life (they're great, but they sure ain't perfect) and your wedding. If your wedding is a reflection of the energy and love you (and perhaps a cast of thousands) have put into it, of course it will inherently be flawed. So what, don't you love those selfsame friends and family in part because of their idiosyncrasies? Sometimes even recognizing that their inconsistencies and imperfections really weren't created simply to annoy you, but that they are, in some very odd way, part of their charm?

Without question, things will go "wrong" on your wedding day. After all, how many times have you looked back on a day and thought that from beginning to end it was absolutely sublime, a thing of utter grace and perfection? Bet you can count those days on one hand. And likely *they* weren't days that involved months of planning.

With wedding-day woes, perspective is nine-tenths of the law, whether it's the wrong flowers on the table or the wrong words out of the officiant's mouth. Here's a stunning example of the latter mishap from bride Michele. "At my wedding ceremony the priest called me Nicole and my husband Jennifer. I kid you not. And this in a Catholic church, no less! At first I was horrified, but my husband was laughing so hard (and trying not to make any sound) that he was shaking uncontrollably. I started laughing silently too, because his laughter is so contagious, but I was secretly hoping nobody noticed. No such luck. People were giggling about it in the receiving line and saying, 'Good night, Nicole' when they left. I did start to feel quite upset about it—because I'd fantasized about the 'Do you, Michele, take Jeff' moment, and now that would never happen. But later when I saw the wedding video and the look on Jeff's face when he was called Jennifer it was so hysterical I couldn't stay upset. We laugh about it to this day."

Laughter is, if not the best remedy, certainly more fun than tears. As for the latter, when it comes to getting weepy over mishaps involving inanimate objects (falling cakes, wilting bouquets, and torn dresses, for example) it's wise to heed the saying "Don't cry over anything that can't cry over you." Of course laughter and tears may have their own happy marriage—for instance, when used in the proper order as a defense against mishaps involving animate objects. (Such as thoughtless words out of the mouth of one of your wedding guests on The Day.) It's called "laugh to keep from crying." Too much to ask? There's also another useful response, called "shrug and move on."

My Big Fat Imperfect Wedding Day

Nightmare: Someone or something will be late, be it the photographer, the ceremony, or your betrothed.

Positive Spin: Gets everyone on the edge of their seats; what's a wedding without a little drama?

Nightmare: Someone gets polluted and says something ludicrous, humiliating, or unbearably maudlin.

Positive Spin: That person licks your boots for years to come. Either that, or you have the perfect excuse never to invite him or her to a party of yours ever again.

Nightmare: Someone gets something terribly wrong—the names on the koala bear glass climbers; the all-beef instead of all-chicken; the location of the wedding.

Positive Spin: You needed some good stories about your wedding day for your grandkids, didn't you?

The Good, the Bad, and the Unmentionable

As anyone who has been to more than one wedding knows, each is like a little pageant unto itself. Even when the wedding in question is as conventionally Princess Bride as can be, there is still room for individuality—given there is always a new set of friends and family, a new range of potentially wonderful or wild dynamics at play. The tales of wedding-day wonders and woes are so numerous and fascinating (at least, for the wedding-obsessed) that one could devote a book to these stories alone. But we won't. Instead, let's hear from three brides with the Cliffs Notes on their respective Big Days.

The Good

Keri tells the story of her "pretty much blissful" wedding like this. "I was overcome with how it felt to be surrounded by so many people who are important in my life. When I came round the corner of my house (I got married in the backyard) and saw everyone, it was a little like a 'Guy Smiley—This Is Your Life' moment. My wedding was smallish, around seventy people, which was great, because it meant everyone there would love me no matter what I did, which stopped me from feeling nervous. I had my nieces and nephews stand up with me (they ranged from two to eight), and they were marvelous. Whatever they say about keeping children out of weddings, they haven't met my gang. The ceremony was beautiful—the minister who married us made an incredible speech; everyone was crying. The toasts had people in tears too. They were all very different, witty, emotional and touching. Then there was the surprise guest, my brother—who was working in South Africa and had said he wouldn't be able to get the time off. When he arrived just before the ceremony he told me, 'I could never forgive myself if I didn't see you get married.' So much for mascara! Then there were all the people who helped out without being asked. One neighbor brought over some beautiful truffles he'd made; another couple let us store wine in their fridge; a neighbor who constructs boats for a living actually built a market umbrella in the days before the wedding since rain was forecast (there was only a sprinkle early on in the day). It's true some small things went wrong—we should have had a microphone for the speeches, for example—but those details really didn't matter. What did matter to me was how people celebrated with us so wholeheartedly, and how affected they were by the wedding. The best proof of that was the next day when a friend called to say she and her boyfriend were so moved by our wedding that they decided to get married too."

The Bad

You may have skipped immediately over The Good to get to this. After all, which is more riveting—happiness or horror? You be the judge. Here's an account of Jamila's wedding day, rather more trying than Keri's. "We've taken to calling it the Murphy's Law wedding," says Jamila. "If a thing could go wrong, it did. First of all there was the whole insanity of my evil dressmaker—which culminated in not getting the dress until the evening before. And when I picked it up she was irritable about having to meet me at night, even though this was totally down to her. She neglected to wish me good luck with the wedding, the only thing she said was it was a pity I'd be wearing the dress outside, which might mean grass stains on her 'creation.' Then the morning of the wedding my maid of honor had stomach flu, and there was no way she could be at the ceremony. Totally upsetting. One of my bridesmaids stepped in, but she was extremely nervous and fainted right before the ceremony, which of course delayed things. (She was fine after that, thankfully!) The ceremony itself was bizarre. The rabbi was absolutely, definitely a little tipsy. At one point he went on this total tangent, a rant really, about the environment and humanity and something about how couples should only have two children given issues of sustainability—which was really nice for us to hear, since we definitely want a big family! Whatever, we got through it. The reception was lovely except when a huge wind came up, and people were holding down the table-cloths, running after their napkins. A bunch of wine glasses were smashed, and the whole catering crew was on their hands and knees picking up glass. Speaking of which, the caterer got the numbers of entrées mixed up, and there were too many vegetarian entrées, so some meat eaters had to go veggie. It really was one minor disaster after another. But for the most part I felt detached from it all. Every-thing seemed dreamlike, kind of surreal. And I was glad about that, I didn't want to be freaking out on my wedding day."

The Unmentionable

Given this dramatic headline, perhaps there should just be a blank paragraph inserted here. However, the fascination with "car-wreck weddings" will not be denied. Fortunately these disastrous wedding days are not the majority, nor even a very vocal minority. Nonethe-less they do exist, leaving all the rest of us in slack-jawed gratitude for our good fortune. Here's Angelica, bold enough to tell all. "My father-in-law and my mother have a totally poisonous relationship. They work in the same industry, and have crossed swords many, many times. The bizarre thing is, my husband and I inadvertently met through them, so it's always been a bit Romeo and Juliet. I remember my mother actually saying once, 'If you go out with him, it's like dating the enemy.' Anyway, we persevered, and when it came to planning the wedding we tried to contain the situation by doing most of the work ourselves, not letting any family members get too involved. It wasn't until the toasts when things went terribly wrong. My father-in-law insisted on toasting us, because despite his feelings about my mother he seems to think I'm a good partner for his son. But partway through his speech my mother stood up and walked out, sweeping half the place settings off the table, you could hear glass breaking. My sisters ran after her, I ran after them. We all ended up in the parking lot. I was crying and furious, and worried—my mother was overwrought. It seemed to mostly be about her feeling I'd betrayed her by letting my father-in-law speak (even though she too had spoken), and also she was convinced something he'd said was aimed at her as a parent—that I'd grown up to be a beautiful woman despite having to struggle. (He was actually talking about a learning disability which I'd overcome, a disability she never likes to acknowledge.) Then in the midst of this melodrama, several of the guests who were friends of my mother's decided to leave. Two of them were trying to console her, when the third managed to smash her car into someone else's van as she was backing out. This brought out a herd of other people who had had much too much to drink— some of them trampled through a flower bed to see what was going on. At this point the manager of the reception facility kind of lost it; he said we were abusing our privileges as guests at his establish- ment. My mother starting yelling at him, saying their job should be to accommodate the emotions of guests on a very emotional day. I ran into the women's room, hysterical myself by this point. Then my husband came in—just walked into the ladies' room. We hugged and both of us started laughing and crying. It was just so over-the-top. Finally we went back in. There were no more speeches. But people tried hard to be positive, coming around and hugging me, and we did actually manage to have fun dancing. My mother came back in but sat as far away as possible from my father-in-law. The wedding ended much earlier than we'd expected."

Imagine. Not pretty. The good news is that Angelica says despite the ongoing tension between the families, she feels she has a happy marriage. Also in the good news department, rest assured the "unmentionable" wedding day is probably about as likely to happen to you as finding yourself strolling beneath a falling piano. That said, doubtless there are aspects of The Big Day that may threaten to make you . . . Go Bridal.

DIAGNOSING THE BIG DAY–INDUCED GOING BRIDAL: THE SYMPTOMS, THE TRIGGERS, THE TREATMENTS, THE GOALS

Symptoms of Big Day–Induced Going Bridal

- The week before your wedding the well-intentioned folks at work greet you by singing "Here Comes the Bride." Instead of playing along, you imperiously announce it's an invasion of privacy, and would they please cease and desist. (Followed by an embarrassed memo of apology for overreacting, after no one even bothers to say good morning the next day.)
- You've completely forgotten your "something blue" the day of, and instead of doing some creative lateral thinking (your eyes, for example, happen to be that shade) you finger your mother's gorgeous blue silk drapes, scissors in hand, insisting to her that no one will ever notice if a corner is missing.
- You're just about to walk down the aisle when you realize you completely forgot to tell the caterer that you wanted the hors d'oeuvres delayed by ten minutes. Shrieking, "The wedding will just have to wait," you gather up your dress and make a mad dash for your cell phone, buried somewhere in your

emergency kit, buried somewhere in the back of your sister's car, buried somewhere in the two hundred–car parking lot.

- The judge taking care of the "Do you take this . . ." business manages to screw up both of your names, so you turn to your assembled guests and audibly hiss, "How hard can it be?"

- Your Aunt Esmeralda tells you she's pleasantly surprised to see that your dress "isn't too bad considering it's not white," and you barely restrain yourself from saying that her face "isn't too bad considering she's on face-lift number three."

- You notice the wedding cake is listing like the Tower of Pisa, and when you cut it a small section plummets. Instead of adopting the "no use crying over spilt cake" approach, you rush at the photographer (knife in hand) insisting she stay an extra half hour to capture the moment . . . once the cake is glued back together.

- Despite the fact that the toasts are long over, a drunken relative grabs the mike and starts telling some barely comprehensible story involving changing diapers (yours) and how you are a stand-in for the kids his ex-wife wouldn't let him have. You find yourself on your hands and knees, bridal dress and all, yanking out the mike power cord.

The Trigger: When Wedding Guests Go Bad

"He/she was like a bad guest at a wedding" is a concept so familiar it has become the standard-bearer of bad behavior for any sort of social occasion. One might justifiably wonder why it is there are so often badly behaved guests at weddings, given weddings are celebrations of love, not celebrations of wing nuts. And yet weddings regularly seem to inspire hell-in-a-handcart/bridge-burning/loose-cannon behavior. The answer to this phenomenon likely lies in the numerous subtexts at weddings, subtexts begging to become the main plot. Typically these stories are about the personal problems belonging to some of the guests, difficulties that may easily be exacerbated when compared to the cozy glow of blissful newlyweds. For some of these precariously balanced attendees, the wedding signals a change not only for the just-wed pair, but for themselves. The loss, perhaps, of a particular chapter in their lives, or of a particular kind of relationship with one member of the loving couple.

Let us be blunt: people's happiness may at times (however unpleasant it is to admit) trigger other people's despair. And it's these sorts of jolly undercurrents that lead all too easily to the "laughter and tears are never far apart," "thin line between love and hate" stuff. Of course in the case of weddings, sometimes the balance between the two is tipped by one of the tried-and-true balance-tippers—booze. It happens in the best of families. Natalie describes her wedding as "a wonderful party," but acknowledges there was indeed a problem of this sort. "It was truly fantastic to see all my friends and family in one place, at one time. After all, when's the next time that will happen? At my funeral—and I won't be there to enjoy it." (Nat's a bit of a card.) "But then there was my brother. He had recently divorced and found the occasion of a wedding extraordinarily painful, and was making every effort to mask his pain. Unfortunately, he chose wine to do so. Despite our strict instructions to the restaurant that we did not wish to exceed the original number of bottles ordered, they eagerly complied with my brother's requests to bring bottle after bottle of fine wine to the table. I think our final tab for wine brought the cost of the dinner to twice what we had originally intended to pay. I did eventually completely forgive my poor brother, and chose instead to blame the mercenary restaurant. My brother was trying so hard to be happy for me—but not succeeding, and sadly it got messy. Why do people always forget that booze is a depressant?"

The Treatment: Delegation

The Goal: So that you do not end up riding herd on every difficult situation that arises on your wedding day, only to discover that when you finally allow yourself to say "At last, I can celebrate," the wedding is over.

The Application: There are many things you may hope to experience on your wedding day. But dealing with wayward guests, even if they are your nearest and dearest, is likely not on that short list. In retrospect Natalie wishes she and her husband had signed a contract with the restaurant limiting the amount—and vintage—of wine that could be served. But she also wishes she'd grasped that she wasn't the best person to solve the brother-on-a-bender debacle. "Throughout most of the evening I kept checking in on my brother, trying to slow him down. Which meant I was totally distracted from the celebration. Later, in the sober light of day, he felt very bad at having taken up so much of my time on my wedding day. Looking back, I wished I'd said to someone else in the family, 'Look, please take care of him, I can't.'"

Natalie's twenty-twenty hindsight is acute. The fine art of delegation is rarely required more than at a wedding. Which isn't to say Natalie should have been prescient and appointed a relative pre-wedding to be her brother's keeper. But as she points out, even in the heat of that thoroughly unpleasant moment, there were other people who could have picked up the sloppy slack.

Some brides take this approach to the entire wedding day by hiring a wedding coordinator as troubleshooter, and this can be a boon. If, that is, you can afford it, and if, that is, you realize your "fixer" likely won't fully understand your family and friend dynamics. The coordinator is probably better equipped to do logistical crisis management. Some brides, feeling this is the case, ask a friend or relative instead of a pro to stage-manage the day. Another possible stress alleviator, but obviously no family member or friend will want to spend all of his or her time at your wedding putting out fires. Still, delegating is key to reducing the amount of running interference you will end up doing versus the amount of hugging, laughing, kissing, crying, sipping, dancing, and thoroughly enjoying your wedding day.

The Trigger: *Who* Did You Say Was at My Wedding?

One of the most common triggers to Big Day–Induced Going Bridal is the sudden, shocking reality of being surrounded by a crush of people you love and who are there to celebrate with you. Despite the fact that this was probably one of the very reasons you decided to have a wedding in the first place, the vision-come-to-life may be overwhelming, causing you to do a minor bit of wig-flipping (a.k.a. Going Bridal). Evelyn found this to be the case. "The frustration lay in having so many people come to a place in my honor, and then feeling this anxiety about not being able to talk to them all. And I admit it, at a certain point I gave up trying. Because I wanted it all: I wanted to visit, I wanted to hostess and make sure everyone had what they needed, I wanted to feel close to my family, and I wanted to have a rip-roaring good time with my friends."

The Treatment: Tough Self-Love

The Goal: So that you end up enjoying your wedding guilt-free, despite having missed talking to Aunt Esmeralda about her gout, or not hearing the play-by-play that resulted in your friend Perpetually-Breaking-Up showing up solo, when just yesterday she was going out with Perfect Wedding Date.

The Application: It helps if you decide in advance, as much as is humanly possible, what you want your wedding day to be—for you. (Well, damnation Missy, who *else* can you actually decide this for?) And once you do decide, you try to stick to that plan. In other words, if you want to be superhostess-with-the-bridal-mostest, spend your time making the rounds, chatting up every person who is eager to have their fifteen minutes of bride. (Even if some of your Best Girls are whining, "Come play with us, already.") Or conversely, if you want to be the I Knew the Bride When She (Still) Could Rock'n'Roll, you party hardy, as they used to say back in the old century, despite disapproving looks and snippy backbiting about how so-and-so didn't get to tell you that you looked radiant. Possibly most challenging is the combo approach—you grant a certain amount of time for decorous visits with your guests, and a certain amount of time to flinging your wedding dress above the knees to kick loose. Whatever your W-Day modus operandi is, it's helpful if you can remind yourself that it is your priority. Not always easy, and Evelyn points out the difficulties. "I think I was a little ideological about wanting it to be just like a fun party and not wanting to be formal about things. If I could do it again I think I would have spent more time playing the role of host. At the same time I wasn't super comfortable being the center of attention so I think I coped as best I could under the circumstances, in the moment."

It's absolutely true that unless you are Elizabeth Taylor (or a close facsimile) you may not know how you will feel until The Day unfolds—given you've never experienced this bride-on-her-wedding-day thing before. That said, having thought about what you *imagine* you'd like is probably better than not having thought about it, period. The head-in-sand approach can be dangerous. It may result on The Day in your reactions popping off like so many champagne corks, eagerly loosened by the cluster of your own personal paparazzi, all wanting a piece of your winning bridal self.

The Trigger: Details, Details
Out of the mouths of brides:

Avril: "The staff was cleaning off the tables during the speeches although we'd asked them to wait until after. Even though it wasn't that loud it took the edge off the moment for me. I kept trying to surreptitiously signal them to stop."

Lynn: "I'd asked the DJ to play some klezmer music for the elders, and he did, but he didn't get the right versions. Every time one of these modern klezmer arrangements was played I could feel myself tensing up instead of letting loose and dancing."

Tamara: "The groomsmen's shoes were all mismatched. I knew I should say 'Who cares?' but after all our efforts to take care of the details it was annoying."

Lina: "The flowers were delivered late, which actually I didn't notice. But it really bugged my mother, and at some point I found it really bugged me."

Andrea: "Even though the wedding is years ago now, I still remember how irked I was when I discovered the hotel had used the wrong salad dressing. Salad dressing!"

Need we say more?

The Treatment: Priorities, Priorities
The Goal: So that you do not spend a speck of unnecessary energy on your wedding day sweating the proverbial small stuff.

The Application: This treatment requires some pregame preparation. Much like a ballplayer practicing mental strategies, you too have to prepare to face The Day "one pitch at a time." And if any of those pitches are deliberately wild, employ self-restraint so that you do not race out to the mound to rip the pitcher's head off, thus getting thrown out of the game.

If you are of a temperament where you may well Go Bridal over a detail gone awry (or entirely AWOL) you might be able to curb this tendency by creating a predecided list of priorities. This could be as simple as: (1) Have fun no matter what. (2) Have fun no matter what. (3) Have fun no matter what. Nora personalized this approach with what she calls the "Three Ps." "I decided to have three priorities that I would recall when any details turned out wrong, because I was pretty sure that would inevitably happen. So my Three Ps were 'be poised, be polite, be professional.' Maybe the last one seems a little strange, but I figured that if I acted as I would hope to act when I'm at my job, no matter what kinds of issues came up on the logistical front, those issues wouldn't send me over the top."

Nora, by the way, runs a theater, where many a backstage slip is the order of the day. But even if you run nothing more stressful than the photocopy machine (which is not to say those damn things can't provide their own brand of stress!) you can apply the same principles, perhaps devising your own triumvirate. For instance, "be pleasant, be powerful, be peripatetic" could serve you just as well.

The Trigger: What Were They Thinking?

Just as weddings seem to create the ultimate "bad guest," they are also conducive to inspiring people to say and do the damnedest things. Sometimes, as was the case for Sheila, the wedding day itself starts out with such an event. "My best friend, who was also my witness, was supposed to meet me for breakfast on my wedding day, just the two of us, a kind of farewell to our single-girl days and hello to the next chapter of our friendship. First she called in the morning in a big flap, saying she was going to be late. Fine, the wedding was much later in the day, and the preparation was all in hand—it was a very casual wedding. Then she called back to change the breakfast venue to one closer to her place, saying, 'Otherwise I'll probably be even later.' She wouldn't tell me why, she just said she'd explain when she saw me. When we finally met she showed up with this guy in tow from the night before. They'd obviously spent the night together and even found the time to shower together, and now I had to have coffee with him? At least she managed to get rid of him quickly, so we could still have our time together. After he left, though, I just stared at her—I'm sure my jaw was on the pavement. Then I said, 'What were you thinking?' She looked so sheepish that I started to laugh, and we ended up slightly hysterical. I still bug her about it to this day, though."

The Treatment: Laugh to Keep from Crying

The Goal: To remind yourself that a sense of humor conquers, if not all, at least a good portion of the absurd things that may happen on your wedding day.

The Application: Some people uphold the idea that really we can't control our feelings, they are purely visceral reactions to our surroundings and the actions of others. If we could control our emotional reactions they wouldn't be feelings, these pontificators pontificate, they'd be thoughts. The Going Bridal Treatment Center advocates otherwise. Who among us has not experienced that split second of indecision when it's obvious that a certain scenario could go either way—on the one hand ending in the perpetuation of a feud, on the other hand resolving in a truce, for example. In other words, that fragment of time when you know that you actually *do* have a choice. If you laugh it will go one way, if you cry another. If you speak calmly it will go left, if you shriek like a banshee, it goes right. Sheila clearly understood this. "One part of me was absolutely furious. How could she bring along some boy she didn't even know to our special wedding-day brunch? I could have killed her. But I saw the glimmer of humor, and took that route. Partly because I think I knew deep down that if I flipped, what would end up happening? My wedding day would be ruined—I love her, and I wanted her to be there. And I didn't want her to be there with the two of us angry with each other. Besides, it more than paid off. She was so amazing through the whole day, and has never stopped thanking me for being the kind of friend who could laugh at a moment like that."

Pregame Stretching

- *Irrational fear.* "What if they serve ice cream instead of cake?"
- *Going Bridal Code Red.* "How could this possibly happen on my wedding day?"
- *Lateral bend.* "What, no cake? Oh well, let them eat ice cream."

- *Irrational fear.* "What if I'm too tense to enjoy a single minute of the damned thing?"
- *Going Bridal Code Red.* "I think I'm hating my wedding day!"
- *Back bend.* "Why was it I thought I'd enjoy a wedding? Oh yeah, him. There he is, guess I'll go and give him a kiss, to hell with photos with the third cousins twice removed."

- *Irrational fear.* "What if she really does bring my ex as her date?"
- *Going Bridal Code Red.* "Should I kill her first, or him?"
- *Child's pose.* "Go to the can. Sit. Lean forward. Lower head to knees. Breathe deeply. Return to wedding. Get hugged by first person who is there to rejoice."

A DAY, NOT LIKE ANY OTHER

Ah yes, The Big Day. Not the only significant day you will have in your life, of course; in fact there probably have already been a few. Graduation, perhaps, or the day you built a better mousetrap, discovered a cure for the common cold—whatever rates highly in your life to date. Regardless, your wedding day likely is one of the standouts. It is a unique day, unlike any other. Which isn't to say it will be "the happiest day of your life." (What, you only get one?) It also won't likely be the "perfect" day, at least not in the sense that absolutely nothing goes amiss. It may well have more than one minor flaw; it may have several moments you'd prefer to forget. But chances are it will also have many beautiful moments you know you will never, ever forget.

Based on the fleet of brides reporting into Going Bridal HQ, it's clear that letting go of the "happiest day" or the "perfect day" bill of goods is key to unlocking the door of sheer enjoyment you may take in your wedding. Take a word from the brides—it will require humor, compromise, delegation, and possibly mind over matter ("I *will* enjoy myself, I *will*"), but your wedding really can be one glorious day, containing all its mishaps and marvels with something that approaches sheer poetry. And if you feel slightly freakish for having to even grapple with your own tense little bridal self to allow that to happen, perhaps recall that there is a reason to be feeling this degree of intensity. It's not merely angst over the guests from Timbuktu arriving late, your fiancé's cufflinks taking a permanent walk, or cakes tumbling all over the floor. Because unless you are marrying purely for reasons of convenience or immigration there is also that little matter of the commitment you are making. No wonder the day feels profound. It is! But its profundity is a symbol, and like all symbols, what it stands for is ultimately far more important than the symbol itself. It's just a signpost on life's road map, merely pointing the way to the journey ahead. So here's to your marriage! A toast . . . to the bride and groom!

EPILOGUE

POSTWEDDING VIEWS (AND BLUES)

THE PRESENTS ARE UNWRAPPED, the champagne is gone (or gone flat, sadly), the memories are exactly that. Yup, the wedding . . . she's over. Where does that leave you, oh bride? Blissfully honeymooning, or counting the hours to takeoff? Having grudgingly gone back to work the next day, or having resumed your vocation with glee? Could be you're poring over the photos with a smile, or maybe fretfully waiting for those over-deadline prints, the delay making you Go Bridal once more, for old times' sake. Whatever the case may be, one thing is certain—you're no longer planning a wedding.

Huzzah! Free at last, free at last, you may shout. Or perhaps you're still quietly reveling in The Day, recalling every sweet thing that was said and done. You feel a glorious mix of contentment and exhilaration—and relief that you never have to look at another wedding checklist again.

On the other hand, you may not be feeling the big happy sigh at your reentry into "normal" life, nor the sweetness of recollection. You may not be feeling as closely bonded with your new husband as you assumed you would. In fact, you may be feeling distinctly less than Joyous New Bride. And if you're at the bottom end of the bummed-out-bride scale, you're feeling lower than a snake's belly.

It's called the Postwedding Blues. And you've got a right to sing them. After all, think how you felt after other momentous events in your life—a special childhood Christmas or birthday, the weekend after your first nerve-racking days at a much-anticipated job, the morning after you finally went out with Mr. Potentially Right for the first time. So much buildup, so much letdown. High expectations have a way of being followed by low realities.

But sometimes Postwedding Blues are deeper than just a day or two of mild melancholy. One bride, Rosie, had a textbook case of the lowdown and dirty Postwedding Blues. "It hit me as soon as we left for the honeymoon," says Rosie. "Instead of feeling excited, I felt awful, kind of depressed and angry—and I wasn't sure why. Instead of seeming like this fantastic romantic vacation, the honeymoon felt like I was being put on hold. It wasn't the wedding, and it wasn't really married life. I couldn't let myself enjoy it. I was anxious about returning to my job, which sucked. And I knew I wouldn't have the excitement of planning the wedding as a distraction. Also I hadn't lived with my husband before we got married, so I was nervous about what that would really be like. When we came home it was better—I felt like at last, this is what it's all about, real life. But even then I was still pretty up and down for a while."

SYMPTOMS, ONE MORE TIME

The state of mind described by Rosie is not uncommon. The symptoms of Postwedding Blues–Induced Going Bridal amount to this: feeling sad when you think you should feel happy, feeling detached when you think you should feel intimate, feeling like something has ended when you think you should feel as if something has begun. That conflict over beginnings and endings is probably most profound. After all, you *have* left something behind—your life as a single (or at least an unmarried) woman. Not to mention the wedding itself, which may have occupied most of your waking (and sleeping) thoughts for months. You've abruptly dismounted from the wedding-planning carousel, and it might take a little time to get your "land legs" again. Plus "normal life" is now normal life with a husband, which may be a mental gear-shift regardless of whether or not you were already living together. But rest assured, there are coping strategies, stumbled on by many a postpartum bride.

THE BRIDES TELL ALL

Bride Sophia: "If I'm being completely honest, I have to admit part of my slump after my wedding was because I was so focused on the preparations that when they were over, I felt this huge void. And irrationally I felt angry with my husband. He was supposed to be the thing that replaced that void, and yet our marriage didn't instantly take care of the sense of emptiness. Gradually I realized this was ridiculous—I needed to fill the void myself, either just by living my life more fully, or literally by getting involved in some new things. I'd spent so much energy on wedding planning that my life revolved around it, to the exclusion of almost everything else. So I started some volunteer teaching, I spent more quality time with my husband, and I started actively researching career changes, which was something I'd been putting off during the months we were planning the wedding."

If you're the sort of person who took on Operation Wedding Planning with a vengeance, no wonder postwedding you might suddenly feel a sense of loss, of a hole in the fabric of your life. (Even if wedding planning made you Go Bridal!) Taking Sophia's practical advice and recognizing you need some new tangibles in your life (or that you need to deal with some old, neglected items) is definitely a smart move. But sometimes there's another emotional and psychological layer to your postwedding onion. Sal reveals this less-than-fragrant reality.

"I think after the wedding was over and I felt so down, my feelings forced me to face up to something I'd been avoiding—that in some ways I was using the wedding planning to avoid really coming to terms with some things in myself, and some things in my relationship. Deep down I was kind of scared. Some days I felt I wasn't totally sure if I was doing the right thing by marrying, or that I'd be able to uphold the commitment I was making. But once I admitted these were some of my real feelings it actually got easier. I think something changes when you name a fear—when you admit it, it becomes less frightening. I also took some reassurance in realizing that my reasons for marrying were generally pretty good, and it's probably natural to feel some anxiety taking such a big step. And, frankly, some therapy helped."

LIFE AFTER WEDDING

Maybe you never felt a lick of Postwedding Blues. Excellent, move on to some fresh reading material. But if you have, or if you are feeling it now (or if you're just curious about some of your fellow brides), it's essential to recognize you are not a freak! Recall, if you will, who it is that says your wedding will be "the happiest day of your life." Why, that would be romance novels, and the wedding industry itself. No vested interest there, hmmm? There's no doubt that even in our all-things-are-possible era there is still a force field surrounding weddings and marriage that bombards us with ideas about how women *should* feel when they choose to marry. Ironically, the pressures of being told you *should* feel a certain way probably contribute to not feeling that way at all. Still, if you're starting to think "If I didn't have bad luck, I wouldn't have any luck at all," you might want to take stock of some of these blues-mood-shifters.

- *A well-placed cliché.* For instance, "This too shall pass." "Time heals all." (Of course, rather annoyingly, it takes time for time to pass. But it will!)
- *Fessin' up.* You might want to share these feelings you're having with that man you married. He may recognize similar feelings in himself. Or not. Either way, in many instances there's little to be gained in married life by maintaining that stiff upper lip.
- *Best girls, boys, dogs.* Your good friends and companions may be less startled to hear of your state of mind than The Hub, who might think it is a reflection on him that you are anything less than blissful. (That said, "Fessin' Up" still applies!)
- *Bride gets a brand new groove.* Hell, you've already just changed your life by getting married, why not seize the day and kick-start some other dreams, or, gulp, face the possibly unpleasant old business you've been avoiding?
- *"I Knew the Bride When She Could . . ."* And you still can. Getting out into the world on your own terms and doing the things you love doing—for you—is part of your critical bridal path.
- *Seeking the comfort zone.* You may have had one with your fiancé prewedding, you'll probably have a different one as a married couple. The adjustment period to marriage isn't all about you-you-you, it's about two-two-two. Specifically about the two of you seeking your mutual comfort zone. It may take some tossing and turning until that cozy spot is mutually achieved, but fear not—given time, a little effort, and a whole lotta love, pretty much anything is possible.

Bye-Bye (Blues)

Although we hate to say good-bye, we must. With this parting thought. If you're experiencing Postwedding Blues it might not hurt to recall that love, while it may not conquer all, helps pass this time on earth with far more beauty than were it not available to you. Consequently there is something to the old "count your blessings," "silver lining in every cloud" stuff that can help in a low moment. That can ease the transition from capital-W wedding to married life lowercase. You too can boldly go where other women have boldly gone before—leaving the galaxy containing Planet Wedding and gradually settling into another journey—the voyage of being married, right here on planet earth.

Home Remedies for the Perpetually Going Bridal

From "Yes" to "I do" can be a trying journey at times, as the stories in this book have indicated. There are days when wedding planning seems like the puppy that follows you from room to room, so very cute . . . up to a point. When that point is reached, its constant panting presence is annoying as hell. What to do? You may want to consider the following remedies. Some are so thoroughly enjoyable that if applied regularly, they have been known to liberate some brides altogether from the ranks of the Perpetually G.B.

Old Faithfuls

- *Entering the zone.* Sometimes referred to as "vegging out," although professionals prefer to call it "downtime." Either way, tends to involve saggy couches and television screens.
- *Advanced pampering.* Professional or fiancé-administered massage, followed by bath products that are not Epsom salts, wine that is not from a box.
- *(De-)elevating the mind.* Seeking out reading material you might prefer to cover with brown wrapping paper on public transit,

not for its X-rated qualities but for its sheer mindless pleasures. (Or possibly for both, come to think of it.)

- *Dietary requirements.* Will vary from individual to individual, but a comprehensive menu plan will typically include the following: Chocolate. Crunchy, salty, nutrient-absent snacks. Anything thoroughly deep-fried.
- *Fiber-optic therapy.* Involves extensive phone conversations with Best Girls, conversations *not* sandwiched in between weighty decisions over pressed flower place cards versus those with beaded filigree.

Old Faithful treatments tend to be applied in near-isolation— only one person can comfortably fit on the massage table, generally not more than two on the sofa. Consequently, you may also want to explore the following group therapy options.

THE GIRLS ARE BACK IN TOWN

Some call this "female bonding," others see it as "maintaining support networks." In common parlance, "chick nights." They can be as simple as a discreet soiree in the confines of one's parlor, or as lacking in discretion as a paint-the-town-several-shades-of-red blowout.

As well, there are the increasingly popular girls' getaways, spas for those with the dough, fifteen-gals-in-one-hot-tub for those with keys to the cousin's cottage. Chick getaways are also fine substitutes for wedding showers and can negate the need for all that gift-giving, particularly if the chicks in question split the bill on all costs.

THE GLOBAL (BRIDAL) VILLAGE

The Internet has altered wedding planning considerably, in some cases for better, in some for worse. (And much like a marriage, you must expect both when wedded to online planning.) Buying secondhand wedding accoutrements through Internet auction, for instance, might be seen as "for better." Being told by a wedding website you really must purchase the "Just Married" thong for your honeymoon might be perceived as "for worse."

Cyber-land does offer one remedy that works very well for some brides—particularly brides who are isolated and lack a gaggle of gals to talk wedding with, or brides whose gals are heartily sick of such conversations. This remedy allows you to "unbridal" yourself with new friends via message boards on wedding websites. You may find solace in general chitchat, or you may seek specifics. For example, should you wish to find real glass slippers in Topeka, you will likely be able to do so via message boards. Or should you wish to discuss the pros and cons of changing your name or your personality after marriage, ditto.

Websites come and go, of course, but give these stalwarts a try:

- *www.indiebride.com.* "Kvetch," a meeting ground for women who believe there is more to life than weddings. (Even if they do indulge in talking about them nonstop.)
- *www.weddingchannel.com.* Mainstream, but less polluted by excessive bombardment of commercialism than some. Check out "Emotional Support," under "Community."
- *www.frugalbride.com.* "Babbling Brides" provides much lore on cost-cutting, also a great place to meet Canuck brides.

DATE NIGHT

Among the best home remedies is Date Night. All you need is a time, a place, your betrothed, and a heartfelt agreement that you're going to enjoy something that doesn't involve a to-do list. Best destinations are movies, boxing matches, poetry readings, baseball games, and karaoke night. (In other words, any place where intimate conversation is impossible.)

Going Bridal Flick 'n' Lit Club

Some brides find (perversely enough) that it is sheer delight to overindulge in the very subject that is making them Go Bridal—via escaping into fictional weddings and the lives of fictional brides. The following mini–reference library could prove an effective remedy if you are of this bridal ilk.

Wedding Flicks

Should you desire, you could avoid wedding planning altogether by having a lost week or two in which you simply watch the hundreds of wedding-related movies. But likely you just want the occasional fix. If so, you could do worse than Entering the Zone with any of the following rentals:

- *The Philadelphia Story.* Katharine Hepburn, Jimmy Stewart, and Cary Grant. Kate!
- *Four Weddings and a Funeral.* Hugh!
- *Bend It Like Beckham.* Brill!
- *My Big Fat Greek Wedding.* Opaa!
- *Muriel's Wedding.* ABBA!

Wedding Fiction

Weddings have always had their place in literature—think *Pride and Prejudice*, for example. But literature requires concentration, and we don't have that at present. Consequently the following is a quick 'n' dirty short list of some recent bride books which, with due respect, are more bride lite than bride lit.

- *Diary of a Mad Bride*, by Laura Wolf. Exactly as titled.
- *Amanda's Wedding*, by Jenny Colgan. Very bloody Brit chick lit.
- *Otherwise Engaged*, by Suzanne Finnamore. More satiric bite than lite, actually.

- *Isobel's Wedding*, by Sheila O'Flanagan. Satisfyingly undemanding.
- *The Shopaholic Ties the Knot*, by Sophie Kinsella. Frequently described as "unabashedly fluffy," taking the genre one step, um, further.

A FINAL WORD FROM THE BRIDE

Possibly one of the more trivial but sweetest parts of getting married is the realization that not only is it a special time for you and yours, but also for you and yourself. Weddings can provide an instant reason to count your blessings, reflect upon your good fortune, and (let's cut to the chase, shall we) to indulge. When else are you actually able to say "I need a pedicure" with such conviction, for example, or so easily rationalize your addiction to chick lit lite?

Yes, there may be issues of time and money. But where there's a will, there's a way, and there is no greater will than the one belonging to a bride. If Going Bridal is becoming an ongoing state, it is essential to exert that will, not toward arguing over who will sit where on The Day, but to hoisting yourself up by the bridal bootstraps and making sure you take the time you need to relax and savor some of the lead-up to your wedding. As for the moolah, many of the best things in life are, if not free, relatively cheap. Why, some of the remedies as described above cost very little. And with consistent application, it truly is possible that you may reach a new level of bridal consciousness—the one called enjoying yourself, even when you're planning a wedding.